FROM THE APOSTLES' FAITH
TO THE APOSTLES' CREED

From the Apostles' Faith

NEW YORK

to the Apostles' Creed

O. SYDNEY BARR

ASSOCIATE PROFESSOR OF NEW TESTAMENT
THE GENERAL THEOLOGICAL SEMINARY, NEW YORK

OXFORD UNIVERSITY PRESS 1964

To Marylin

CONTENTS

ARTICLE THREE

FROM THE APOSTLES' FAITH
TO THE APOSTLES' CREED

THE APOSTLES' CREED

I believe in God the Father Almighty,
Maker of heaven and earth:

And in Jesus Christ his only Son our Lord:
Who was conceived by the Holy Ghost,
Born of the Virgin Mary:
Suffered under Pontius Pilate,
Was crucified, dead, and buried:
He descended into hell;
The third day he rose again from the dead:
He ascended into heaven,
And sitteth on the right hand of
God the Father Almighty:
From thence he shall come to judge
the quick and the dead.

I believe in the Holy Ghost:
The holy Catholic Church;
The Communion of Saints:
The Forgiveness of sins:
The Resurrection of the body:
And the Life everlasting. Amen.

INTRODUCTION

The first Good Friday was a stunning blow to the followers of Jesus of Nazareth. It was not that they were totally unprepared. He himself had envisaged some such tragic climax and had forewarned them. But even so, there had been high hopes. They had heard his penetrating words, had witnessed his mighty works, and had clung stubbornly to the conviction that through this Jesus, the God of their fathers was mightily at work. The cross, however, was irrevocably decisive. "We *had* hoped that he was the one to redeem Israel" (Luke 24:21, italics mine) — but who could hope now?

And then, suddenly, the whole picture changed. "The third day he rose again from the dead!"

Was this mere wishful thinking, taking the optimistic view, making the best of things? Such explanations are not sufficient to explain the creation of the New Testament, nearly two thousand years of Church history, and millions of changed lives. Nor do such explanations square with the biblical evidence. For the New Testament witness to the Resurrection points to an indubitable fact — that after Good Friday the first Christians continued to know Jesus as present in their midst, present more intimately and meaningfully even than during the earthly ministry. God's mightiest deed of all time had overcome the cross.

It had overcome all the fears and doubts of his followers, too. Suddenly, irresolution and frustration gave way to joy. The scattered disciples came together again as a purposeful missionary Church. In the very city where he had been crucified and from which they had fled, the word went forth: this Jesus whom Judas betrayed, whom Peter denied, whom the disciples, all hopes gone, had deserted — this one God has raised from the dead (Acts 2:22-36)! And ever since that time the cross of shame has been proclaimed as God's way of strength and hope and life, and he who died upon it as the Son of God. "We preach Christ crucified," wrote St. Paul some twenty years later, "a stumbling-block to Jews and folly to Gentiles, but to those who are called, both Jews and Greeks, Christ the power of God and the wisdom of God" (I Cor. 1:23,24).

These are all things which are a matter of record and verifiable by the historian. Certain words and actions of Jesus, the puzzled hope of his followers, his Crucifixion and their despair, the absolute certainty that God had raised him, the jeers of non-believers, the complete about-face of his disciples' lives, the beginning of an aggressive Christian Church — these things actually happened.

But what of Paul's witness that the crucified Jesus is "the power of God and the wisdom of God"? What of the Church's testimony that Jesus is God's own Son? This is faith's response, faith's answer as to the ultimate significance of those things which the historian can demonstrate.

Our own lives are indissolubly linked with certain concrete phenomena and events. We ask "why" and "how," we search for meaning. Out of the context of such knowledge and experience that we already possess, we try to fit those things which impinge upon us from the outside into the total fabric of history. In such manner, also, and because to ask questions is the way to understanding, we make each particular event more truly and intimately a part of our own personal history. This is our response.

4

So, too, the first Christians asked questions and sought for the meaning of the event which had happened to them, Jesus of Nazareth. They had companied with him, seen and heard him, observed him from afar as he walked to his death. But more than this, the impact of his life upon their lives had not lessened but intensified beyond measure after that black Friday. They became, almost in spite of themselves, new people. What, they asked, does this all signify — about him, about us, about the world in which we live? And their answer was Paul's answer — that in and through Jesus, God had acted powerfully and climactically to make Himself known, to complete His creation, and to save.

Such, then, was the response given by faith, the Christian gospel, the "good news" or "glad tidings" which went forth from Jerusalem to the whole world. And it remains the Church's witness today.

If a Christian were asked, "What do you believe?" he would be quite correct in handing his interlocutor a copy of the Bible: "Here is your answer." But the Bible is a long and in many ways difficult book. It would be far better as a beginning to point one's inquirer to the Apostles' Creed: "Here is our faith as Christians." For the Creed is a summary of the biblical faith.

This summary, however, is a *minimal* one — the distilled essence of the biblical witness, and of that which a person must profess if he would claim the name "Christian." As a skeletal structure, it must be clothed if one is to apprehend its affirmations as "saving" facts. We must after all, then, go back to Holy Scripture. For it is there that one finds the earliest and chief witness as to what the first followers of Jesus believed, and why.

In the Bible, however, one finds no Apostles' Creed — not,

at least, in any easily recognizable form. A quick turning of the pages makes this clear. Jesus delivered no official formulary to his adherents. And in the New Testament period, during, that is, the first hundred years or so of the Church's life, our Creed in anything like its present shape simply did not exist.[1] For that matter, it did not attain to the precise form which it has now before the eighth century. What, then, is its connection with Holy Scripture?

As far as chronology is concerned, we can immediately eliminate most of the time gap between the eighth century formulary and biblical times. For the Apostles' Creed is a direct descendant of the "Old Roman Creed" which was current among Christians at Rome not long after A.D. 150.[2] With the exception of a few phrases, mainly in the third Article, these two are virtually identical.

The matter of dating, however, is relatively unimportant. What of concepts, content, language? It is here that the relationship between Creed and Scripture becomes so apparent.

The tripartite construction, for example, of both the Apostles' Creed and its second-century ancestor, is biblical. The "Old Roman Creed" was used chiefly as a Trinitarian baptismal confession of faith. Immediately, one thinks of the dominical command recorded by Matthew: "Go therefore and make disciples of all nations, baptizing them in the name of the Father and of the Son and of the Holy Spirit" (28:19). Here are the three Articles of the credal format: "I believe in God . . . in Jesus Christ . . . in the Holy Ghost. . . ."

This framework, however, has been filled in with certain key historical and theological affirmations which, for the Christian, demand confession of God as Holy Trinity. And it is in these, especially, that we can see the Creed's biblical roots. For both the content and the phraseology of our formulary are strik-

[1] See Appendix I. The last book of the canonical New Testament to have been written is II Peter, A.D. 130–150.
[2] See Appendix II.

6

ingly similar to that of the New Testament witness to the faith of the earliest Church. The Apostles' Creed, as we shall see, though not appearing *per se* in Holy Scripture, is nevertheless deeply rooted in the biblical record.

The closeness of this relationship can be underlined in another way: both Creed and New Testament are Apostolic Witness, the same witness. And we mean, here, eyewitness — for Jesus had followers who were the nucleus of all that happened later. These included more than the handful who stayed with him until the night of the betrayal. There were many others who had followed for a time, and then gone their way, but finally, when his Resurrection was proclaimed, hailed him as the Christ. They, too, played a key role in the primitive community's recalling of the past, their new lives a result of, and witness to, Jesus' words and deeds. These were the ones who initially asked, "Who is he? What is the meaning of the wonder which has happened to us?" It was they who first found the answers which propelled Christianity into a worldwide religion. And it is in them that the Church's faith, now over nineteen centuries old, has its origin, and so is called the *Apostolic* Witness. Furthermore, because it is rooted in the experience of those who were there, it merits serious consideration as a special authority.

But it is the same witness that is summarized for us in the Creed. It too, then, is a special authority, and, understandably, has been recognized as a cornerstone of the Church's life from earliest times. To be sure, the ancient account, which tells us that each of the twelve Apostles in formal assembly contributed one statement to the Creed, is a legend. Yet, like many such stories, this one contains an important core of truth — that our present formulary, allowing, of course, for expansions which were the inevitable and necessary result of continuing Christian experience, preserves and mediates that identical faith which was preached almost two thousand years ago. The *Apostles'* Creed, we call this summary, and appropriately so. Because it is *Apostolic* Witness — the testimony of those who were there — which it proclaims.

What, now, is the essential character of the Apostolic Witness? The answer, in brief, can be summed up in one phrase. It is a "double witness." This is of special importance, because it is a key to one's understanding and use of Bible and Creed alike.

The past hundred years or so have made available an impressive body of new knowledge with respect to Holy Scripture. One insight of particular value is the recognition that these books preserve for us not simply historical data, but vivid faith as well.

In the pages of the Old Testament, for example, we read the story of a real-life people. Here is the record of certain specific facts which the historian can verify — particular calendar events, wars and famines and times of plenty, kings and priests and prophets — all the things, that is, which constituted the ongoing life of Israel's existence as a part of the near-Eastern world.

We read more than this, however — the deep meaning which this people found in their history. There was, they believed, more to day-by-day existence than mere hand-to-mouth living. With special vividness, they discerned every experience, every concrete reality of national and personal life, as an encounter with the God who is Lord of all history. And so, with an intertwining of myth and poetic imagination, the Old Testament avows a dimension of reality with respect to Israel's existence which the historian cannot verify. Here, that is, we have *sacred* history, this people's past and present told not as a barren statistic, but viewed "under God."[3]

It is *sacred* history, a "double witness," which we read in the

[3] See further below, pp. 32–43.

New Testament, too. Christianity began with certain indubitable historical events which took place "under Pontius Pilate." The New Testament is a record of those events — the existence of one Jesus of Nazareth, the basic pattern of his life and ministry, his chief concerns, certain things he said and did, in short, things that people actually saw and heard.

But the witness goes far deeper than the recording of such data. Every page is "gospel," the good news that there is far more than meets the eye to that brief span of thirty or so years in Galilee and Judea. The Apostolic Witness tells us what those who were actually on the spot, and their converts, believed about this Jesus. Nor, to learn what that response was, do we have to confine ourselves solely to the few texts where a writer says specifically, "we believe," or something equally obvious.[4] The practices and worship of the primitive Church, her missionary expansion, her struggles against disbelief and persecution, the intimate lives of her members — all these elucidate the faith of the first Christians, all were created by the original event, and so, in turn, say important things about its (and his) significance.

This, then, is what we mean by "double witness" — the New Testament has not only preserved for us facts, but also has interpreted them, and testified over the centuries that they have a meaning so deep as to defy adequate human description. This had all been God's doing "for us men and for our salvation" — for the first believers who had encountered that history, and whose lives had been upturned by it, here was the one answer that sufficed. And in diverse and, oftentimes, paradoxical and highly imaginative ways — is this not inevitable, when we attempt to describe and explain realities which are too great for us? — using the thought forms and word pictures of their culture and their day, they shouted their faith.

The fact that we are here dealing with sacred history has two practical consequences of the greatest significance. In the

4 Rom. 10:9; I Cor. 15:2; I Th. 4:14; etc.

first place, we are delivered from the unrealistic insistence that every utterance of Jesus was spoken precisely as recorded in the tradition. Nor do we have to assume that every action or event occurred exactly as described. There is need, therefore, neither for sense of strain, nor for negative defensiveness in our use of the biblical sources.

Second, and equally important, we are free to accept the entire tradition. For example, those accounts of activities which, taken literally, are for many today more puzzling than meaningful, we can embrace wholeheartedly. For we know that everything in our sources was ultimately impelled by Jesus, and that everything points back to him and says something important about him.

All that we have been asserting about the scriptural witness can be applied as well to its summary, the Apostles' Creed. It, too, is sacred history. To recite its words is to recall, and make one's own, that same Apostolic Witness which is preserved in the New Testament. Some would simply avoid or slough off some of the affirmations that seem strange or difficult. But there is no need for this; nor, for that matter, can we do so, because all of the credal witness is rooted in Christian origins, not just part. Jude's description of the Church's faith as something "once for all delivered to the saints" contains much truth (vs. 3). Of course, presuppositions, techniques, and knowledge are constantly changing. Each successive generation, then, must address its own questions to that faith, and seek new ways of publishing its good tidings. But for all that, it is the *same* witness and the *same* Lord which are proclaimed: "Jesus Christ is the same yesterday and today and for ever" (Heb. 13:8). And it is by accepting and understanding the Apostolic Witness in its totality that Christ is most fully known.

In the pages that follow we shall be examining the Apostles' Creed phrase by phrase. And in connection with each, we shall pose such questions as these: What in the life and teaching of Jesus throws light upon these words? What in turn do they tell us about him? Why, and in what sense, did they become an integral part of the Apostolic Witness?

We shall not by this means have exhausted the meaning of the Creed in contemporary Christian thought. Only a study of the history of each phrase, and of the theology which centers on it, over the long span of the centuries would make a complete exposition possible. But to understand the role played by these credal affirmations in the lives of the earliest believers in New Testament times adds much to one's understanding of the Christian faith in its wholeness.

The writer of Hebrews reminds us that "faith is the assurance of things hoped for, the conviction of things not seen" (Heb. 11:1). The Creed begins with the words, "I *believe*," and this phrase is no less important than what follows. The Church's witness is to a kind of truth which, in the final analysis, each individual has to authenticate for himself in his or her own daily living.

But *why* and *how* did the Church come to proclaim Jesus Christ as God's unparalleled action in His world? Here is something which *can* be demonstrated. From the very beginning, Christians have had reasons for what they believe. The more clearly we can see this "why" and "how" of the Apostolic Witness, the better will be our understanding of the "why" and "what" of the Church's life today. And to search the Scriptures is the indispensable first step.

I

ARTICLE ONE

I believe in God,
the Father,
Almighty,
Maker of heaven and earth.

I

Introduction

"I believe in *one* God . . ." states the longer Nicene Creed and, of course, *oneness* is assumed by our shorter formulary. It was the God of monotheistic Judaism who had sent His Messiah and revolutionized the lives of Jesus' followers.

This immediately introduces us to a foundation stone of Christian origins. Both Jesus and his closest adherents were Jews. It was out of this background that they thought and spoke, using the imagery of Judaism, and Palestinian Aramaic, the street dialect of their day. Christianity is gratefully and proudly and inseparably linked with this past. Unless this fact is recognized and welcomed, one cannot understand the "why" and the "what" of the Church's faith. There will be many illustrations of this as we go on. Briefly, now, we turn to something quite different.

For the Christian, God's oneness is a unity of three Persons: Father, Son, Holy Spirit. The Nicene Creed, particularly in its second and third Articles, affirms this explicitly.[1] In the Apostles' Creed, we recognize it as an implication of the tripartite format. Trinitarianism as a theological concept is beyond the province of this study. For that matter, as something

[1] See Appendix III.

15

consciously thought out, it does not appear in the New Testament. We can, however, point to its beginnings.

Most obvious is the command cited by Matthew to baptize "in the name of the Father and of the Son and of the Holy Spirit" (28:19). These are Church words, an early baptismal formula attributed to Jesus. They show us that some years prior to the final decade of the first century Trinitarianism was developing.[2] And almost forty years earlier, the Apostle Paul used a tripartite benediction formula at the end of one of his letters: "The grace of the Lord Jesus Christ and the love of God and the fellowship of the Holy Spirit be with you all" (II Cor. 13:14).

But more important is the fact that Jesus' entire life and ministry exhibit this "threeness." We shall be discussing in other connections his stress upon *God as Father,* his understanding that his special vocation to *Sonship* was something crucial to God's plan for the world, and his conviction that in and through his ministry God's *Spirit* was as never before active on the plain of history. This is not Trinitarianism as we know it. But it is an indispensable foundation stone for the later theological development.

The same "threeness" of single divine activity is apparent in the convictions of his first followers. Jesus, they declared, was the one whom *God* had promised would come, His *Messiah.* And to acknowledge him as such was to know a newness of life which they could do no less than ascribe to the activity of the divine *Spirit.*

This is vastly to oversimplify a complex matter. However — and this is our only concern here — between the life and teaching of Jesus, the Apostolic Witness of the primitive Church, and Trinitarian theology, there is a clear line of continuity. And it is because this is so that the Church's baptismal formula could be and was, as happened in Matthew 28:19, attributed to Jesus himself. The "threeness" was present from the very

[2] Matthew's Gospel is usually dated A.D. 85–100.

beginning: the historical event *Jesus* of Nazareth was *God's* supreme *activity* for and in His world!

II

One God

After his Ascension Jesus' followers "with one mind . . . kept up their daily attendance at the temple, and, breaking bread in private houses, shared their meals with unaffected joy, as they praised God and enjoyed the favour of the whole people . . ." (Acts 2:46 f.; N.E.B.). These words underline two facts with respect to Christianity: it was (and is) at one and the same time something *old* and something *new*.

The disciples, Luke tells us, reassembled in Jerusalem (Acts 1:4, 12 f.).[1] They continued, as had been their custom before the Crucifixion (more than once in company with Jesus himself) to worship in the Jewish manner in the Jerusalem temple. At first there was little to distinguish them from their contemporaries aside from the all-important conviction that God's Messiah had indeed come. And for this, and for the "unaffected joy" which it occasioned, they "praised God" — not, however, a different God, but He whom they had always known. It was, Peter declares, "the God of Abraham and of Isaac and of Jacob, the God of our fathers" who had reversed the human judgment of the cross (Acts 3:13). Here was the *oldness*.

But there was *newness,* too. Jesus himself had said, "no one puts *new* wine into old wineskins . . . new wine is for fresh skins" (Mark 2:22, italics mine). Paul, who had been overwhelmed by the risen Jesus on the road to Damascus, knew the truth of these words and wrote some twenty years later,

1 The Evangelist Luke is also the author of the Acts of the Apostles.

"Therefore, if any one is in Christ, he is a new creation; the old has passed away, behold, the new has come" (II Cor. 5:17). And here in our text from Acts that *newness* which was soon to distinguish Christianity from Judaism shines through in the phrase "breaking bread in private houses."

These words probably refer to an embryonic form of the Christian Eucharist. In any event, even as the old ways continued, already in the first weeks there were distinctively *Christian* gatherings and the beginnings of a distinctively *Christian* worship. Messiah had come! And things could not be, and were not, the same as before.

The *oldness* is important. So, too, is Christianity's Jewish heritage, and strikingly illustrated by this first Article. We have but to look at the teaching of Jesus and of his followers.

"Which commandment is the first of all?" With these words a certain scribe sought to test Jesus' orthodoxy (Mark 12:28). If the questioner had any expectation of hearing something new, he was quickly disillusioned. For without a moment's hesitation Jesus replied by reciting the "Shema":

> The first is, "Hear, O Israel: The Lord our God, the Lord is one; and you shall love the Lord your God with all your heart, and with all your soul, and with all your mind, and with all your strength." The second is this, "You shall love your neighbor as yourself." There is no other commandment greater than these (Mark 12:29-31).

The "Shema" was (and is today) Judaism's primary confession of faith.[2] And the scribe's reply shows that Jesus had indeed met the challenge: "You are right, Teacher; you have truly

[2] Technically, the "Shema" included only the first part of Jesus' reply, the reference, that is, to love for God. In its entirety, the formula in time came to include Dt. 6:4-9, 11:13-21, and Num. 15:37-41. The second commandment which Jesus cited comes from Lev. 19:18. It has been thought by some, improbably, that Jesus was the first to combine these two commandments. How-

18

said that he is one, and there is no other but he" (Mark 12:32).

For that matter, much of what Jesus said and did passed the "orthodoxy test." His fundamental task was to preach not a new religion, but the gospel of that God whom he, like his Jewish forefathers, in synagogue and temple addressed as "Almighty," "Father," "Creator." Good news from this same God, glad tidings about this same God — these were his sole concern.

But what was the good news? Mark's Gospel summarizes it for us; the words may be those of Jesus himself: "The time is fulfilled, and the kingdom of God is at hand" (1:15). There was, however, nothing unorthodox about this. Every pious Israelite for years and years had yearned for the Kingdom. Others before, and most recently John the Baptist, had hailed its imminence. Every hearer knew, or thought he did, just what Jesus meant, and thrilled at his words.

And after the Resurrection believers likewise hailed and rejoiced in the Kingdom's dawning, proclaimed their master as God's Messiah bringing it to fulfillment, and were certain that it was the new life of the Kingdom which they were presently living empowered by the outpouring of the Spirit promised for the "last days" (Acts 2:1–36). In other words, that which was coming to pass was the accomplishment of Judaism's fondest hopes.

What did this all mean in terms of one's daily living? Again we recall the answer to the inquiring scribe: "You shall love your neighbor as yourself" (Mark 12:31). So Jesus summarized the ethic of the Kingdom in words almost as old as Judaism itself. To let God be King is to do His holy will, which is to love.

The earliest Christian ethic likewise had Jesus' summary at its center. "Owe no one anything, except to love one another;

ever, Lev. 19:18 was frequently used in the Judaism of the day as a summary of man's ethical obligation. Moreover, to recall the humaneness of the Deuteronomic Code and of Jewish ethical teaching in general, and the sternness of the prophetic denunciations in God's name against the sins of His people, is to recognize that "love God and love neighbor" were an integral part of Israel's covenant obligation.

for he who loves his neighbor has fulfilled the law" (Rom. 13:8). The Christian life is faith in Christ dynamically asserting and realizing itself through love (Gal. 5:6).[3]

We do not forget the other side of the picture. Jesus was highly critical of not a little within Judaism, and categorically abrogated or modified more than one of its provisions.[4] Moreover, although the content of his ethical teaching was not strikingly original, the imperiousness of its demand and its radical application were. To all intents and purposes, the divine will for man had already been revealed in the law and the prophets. But Jesus proclaimed it with an unheard-of strenuousness. God's will *must* be done.

Even more significant is the fact that Jesus' own manner of life was a dramatic representation of his words, the very "incarnation" of what God's sovereign will means for human life — in terms of concern, judgment, forgiveness, and love as a power which makes whole and saves. Indeed, there was *newness*.

But the origin of all this in Judaism's centuries-old struggle to know and to follow the one God is manifest. Jesus proclaimed that Israel (and all God's world) *must* be that which she had long since been called to be.

III

Almighty, Maker of Heaven and Earth

It is, then, Israel's God whom the first Article acknowledges. And other phrases in this affirmation — "Almighty, Maker of heaven and earth" — remind us of this fact. For that matter,

[3] See also I Cor. 13:13; Gal. 5:14; Col. 3:14; John 15:12; I John 4:7–21.
[4] Matt. 5:21–48; Mark 2:18–3:6; 7:1–13; etc.

the New Testament is full of such confessions and paeans of praise. Here are a few examples:

the Most High (Luke 1:76)

The God who made the world and everything in it, being Lord of heaven and earth (Acts 17:24)

to the only God . . . be glory, majesty, dominion, and authority, before all time and now and for ever. Amen. (Jude 25)

the blessed and only Sovereign, the King of kings and Lord of lords (I Tim. 6:15)

These and innumerable others represent direct borrowings by Christians, who had in many cases been born and reared in Judaism, from the rich store of the liturgy of temple and synagogue.

Present-day liturgical usage reflects the same unbroken tradition. In ancient times, the Church used as her own the Jewish hymnal, that is, the Psalms, which remain today a backbone of the Daily Offices in the Anglican and Roman obediences. And Christian liturgies generally are replete with words which were familiar to every Israelite of Jesus' day. These examples from the Book of Common Prayer are typical:

Heaven and earth are full of the Majesty of thy glory (p. 10)

Blessed art thou, O Lord God of our fathers: praised and exalted above all for ever (p. 11)

HOLY, HOLY, HOLY, Lord God of hosts, Heaven and earth are full of thy glory: Glory be to thee, O Lord Most High (p. 77)

All glory be to thee, Almighty God, our heavenly Father (p. 80)

21

Our Father, who art in heaven, Hallowed be thy Name
(p. 7, *passim*)

The first Article, then, is a striking reminder of Christian origins. Its every word was repeatedly on the lips of Jesus himself. This is again to underline the fact that, without a recognition which welcomes this Jewish heritage, it is impossible to understand or appreciate the depths of subsequent Church history and experience.

IV

The Father

The first Article, for all its being rooted in the past, is a *Christian* confession. And "Father," although also a Hebraic title for deity, underlines this fact. It has, of course, a complement in the phrase "Son of God" in the second Article. We must, then, look at its history in some detail.

The Jewish worshiper addressed God as both "King" and "Father." The ascription of kingship underlined His role as transcendant and omnipotent Creator and Ruler of the entire world. The title "Father," however, expressed quite another aspect of God's sovereignty. In early Hebrew tradition, kingship retained much of its original local and provincial flavor. The king, somewhat like the desert tribal head, was closely associated with his people, his own welfare intimately connected with theirs. This note of intimacy was never lost. Hence, God omnipotent and transcendant was at the same time thought of as an intensely personal being, knowing and knowable in immediate personal relationship.

These different perspectives are apparent in the liturgical

patterns of Jesus' day. On the one hand, His majestic "wholly-otherness" was extolled in phrases such as "the most high God," "holy art thou and terrible is thy name," and others of the kind noted previously. At the same time, and with no sense of contradiction, Jesus and his contemporaries prayed, as one person to another, "Bless us, our Father," or in words which recall the Lord's Prayer, "Forgive us our Father, for we have sinned against Thee."

Jesus, then, was not the first to use the title "Father." It was, however, especially characteristic of his teaching. Phrases such as "your Father," "sons of your Father," "your heavenly Father" were frequently on his lips (Matt. 5:16, 45; 6:32). Moreover, his use of the word had many nuances. The parable of the Prodigal Son pictures that kind of forgiveness which is born of a father's (God's) love (Luke 15:11–32). Or in the parables of the Lost Sheep and the Lost Coin, God is depicted as one who with yearning seeks his own (Luke 15:3–10). If imperfect human fathers ("you . . . who are evil") will not give a stone to the son who asks a loaf, "how much more will your Father who is in heaven give good things to those who ask him" (Matt. 7:7–11)? And the Lord's Prayer is virtually a command to call God "Father."

But Jesus also addressed God as his own Father. His baptism in the river Jordan, according to tradition, was accompanied by a heavenly voice which affirmed, "Thou art my beloved Son; with thee I am well pleased," an assurance and witness that were repeated on the Mount of Transfiguration (Mark 1:11; 9:7; II Peter 1:17 f.). At the end of his ministry, in the Garden of Gethsemane he prayed, "Abba, Father . . . remove this cup from me" (Mark 14:36). On the cross he pleaded, "Father, forgive them," and with his last breath declared, "Father, into thy hands I commit my spirit" (Luke 23:34, 46). The question, "Did you not know that I must be in my Father's house?" suggests how early (Jesus is reputed to have been twelve years old at the time) and keenly he may have come to think of his relationship with God in terms of fatherhood and sonship (Luke 2:49).

Jesus' use of this title is highly expressive of his central message. God is King; the world of men *must* give way to His sovereignty. The father, of course, in Judaism was an authoritative figure. To call God "Father" is to admit His sole authority, to accept total dependence upon His willingness to give, and to obey His will. And this is precisely what Jesus wished for his hearers.

Even more important, however, is the striking manner in which he lived this divine imperative. It is this which makes his use of "my Father" of particular importance. For the observed fact of Jesus' own life of conscious and effectual closeness to God was one of the basic elements that led Christians at an early date to confess him as divine Son.[1]

"Begone, Satan! for it is written, 'You shall worship the Lord your God and him only shall you serve'" (Matt. 4:10). Thus in the desert wilderness at the beginning of the ministry, he determines that his own life must be given totally to God's service if he is to demand of others complete submission to the divine kingship: "I am among you as one who serves"; "You cannot serve God and mammon" (Luke 22:27; Matt. 6:24). So a son submits to his father's supremacy, and does only his will.[2]

Or we may note the authoritative certainty with which Jesus speaks and acts: "You have heard that it was said to the men of old . . . But I say to you"; "What is this? A new teaching! With authority he commands even the unclean spirits, and they obey him" (Matt. 5:21–48; Mark 1:27). So a son exercises the authority which his father may give him.

Also significant is Jesus' equation of loyalty to himself with that complete submission which God demands: "So every one who acknowledges me before men, I also will acknowledge

[1] See below, pp. 64–76, and particularly pp. 66 f.
[2] This analogy postulates the patriarchal society of Jesus' day, as well as the best of "sons" and the best of "fathers."

before my Father who is in heaven"; "For whoever does the will of my Father in heaven is my brother, and sister, and mother"; "come, follow me" (Matt. 10:32; 12:50; Mark 10:21). So a son makes known the will and the way of his father.

The authority with which Jesus performed his mission, the complete trust with which he faced suffering and death, the certainty with which he looked forward to the future — all reflect an unqualified and unparalleled obedience and dependence upon God, as a son upon a father, intimate knowledge of the divine will and purpose, absolute certainty of a commissioning from above. Matthew's Gospel expresses it this way:

> All things have been delivered to me by my Father; and no one knows the Son except the Father, and no one knows the Father except the Son and any one to whom the Son chooses to reveal him (Matt. 11:27; cf. Luke 10:22).

These words, at least in this particular form, are largely the Church's meditative reflection upon the earthly ministry. So too is the saying in the Fourth Gospel, "I and the Father are one" (10:30). Such "theologizing" was the necessary task of the later Church. But we have here words which are essentially authentic — for Jesus' own use of filial imagery with respect to himself and God reflects an awareness of "oneness," "identity," to which every aspect of his earthly ministry bears witness.

Specifically, now, what of the early Church's use of "Father"? Immediately one is struck by the correspondence with Jesus' own practice and teaching.

He, for example, had repeatedly spoken of God as his own Father. With this in mind, look now at these words: [3]

> Blessed be the God and *Father of our Lord Jesus Christ* (II Cor. 1:3; cf. Eph. 1:3).

[3] Italics mine.

The God and *Father of the Lord Jesus,* he who is blessed for ever (II Cor. 11:31).

We always thank God, *the Father of our Lord Jesus Christ* (Col. 1:3).

Early Christians, especially in their worship, followed the pattern set during the earthly ministry and hymned God as the Father of Jesus.

In these texts we find *old* and *new* side by side. The ascription "Blessed be God," as we have already seen, is typical Jewish prayer language.[4] But it has been taken over and filled with a new content — by the simple expedient of using that epithet of the one God of Judaism which was most frequently on Jesus' own lips, "Father." This seemingly insignificant phenomenon says much. Jesus had invoked God as "my Father." And his life of obedient sonship had given that title a new dimension of meaning. To know God as the "Father of Jesus" (the Jesus who at the same time was confessed as Messiah and divine Son!) was to have a new vision of deity.

But Jesus had as well enjoined that all invoke God, and let Him rule in their lives, as "Father." And the result we can see in the refrain which recurs, almost word for word, in the opening lines of numerous New Testament epistles:[5]

Grace to you and peace from God *our Father* and the Lord Jesus Christ (Rom. 1:7).

As with the previous examples, here too current Jewish liturgical practice ("the peace of God," "peace be with you") has been taken over by the Church. The "Christianizing" has been accomplished by setting God and Christ side by side as the source of grace and peace. But the *newness* is also under-

[4] Twice, for example, Paul cites, without "Christianizing," the Jewish formula of blessing which lies behind these words: ". . . the Creator, who is blessed for ever! Amen"; "God who is over all be blessed for ever. Amen" (Rom. 1:25; 9:5).

[5] I Cor. 1:3; II Cor. 1:2; Eph. 1:2; Phil. 1:2; Pm. 3; Gal. 1:3; Col. 1:2; cf. II Th. 1:2; I Tim. 1:2; II Tim. 1:2; Tit. 1:4. Italics mine.

lined by the "God *our Father*" which stands as a perpetual reminder of Jesus' injunction. And again, behind the title in these Christian contexts lies all that Jesus taught by word and deed about the Fatherhood of God. Because of him, God is known as never before.

We have been thinking in terms of *oldness* and *newness*. And this — to say the same thing in a different way — is to note that earliest Christian faith had two foci, God and Christ. The texts which we have just been discussing are a good example of this "bipolarity." God and Christ are hymned side by side. Jesus, as Messiah, is the long-awaited fulfillment of the promises made long ago by Judaism's God. And it is faith in that one God that the Messiah's coming has underscored.

But there is another way of looking at it. There was but *one* fact, the conviction that Jesus was the Messiah, which at first distinguished Christians from their fellow Jews. It was because of refusal to desist from so proclaiming him that some of them were persecuted in Jerusalem.[6] The same overwhelming certainty impelled them, with a missionary zeal unknown to Judaism, to proffer the good news to Gentiles. In short, the fact that the Messiah had come was a *newness* which the old could not contain, so that Christianity obviously and soon went its own way. Viewed from this perspective, there was but one focus. It was Christ who made the difference.

The texts just cited above illustrate this, too. Here the word "Father," used as Jesus himself employed it, is the key, underlining the *newness,* the "unipolarity" of the earliest faith. As an example, note again II Corinthians 1:3 cited earlier. We may paraphrase these words as follows:[7]

[6] Acts 4:3, 18–22; 5:17–32; 6:8–15; 7:54–60; 8:1–3; 9:1 f.; 12:1–5; etc.
[7] Actually, this is to change but one word, the Greek "kai," substituting "even" for "and." Syntactically this is possible, and the Authorized Version so renders it.

Blessed be God, *even* [He who is, whom we now know above all else to be] the Father of our Lord Jesus Christ. . . .

In other words, it is His Fatherhood of Jesus which has become the most important thing about God. Jesus is the *newness,* the focal point. His use of "Father" is a fresh revelation with respect to the one God of Judaism. And for the Jew, if he would but accept Jesus' messiahship, no less than for the Gentile, the words and works of the prophet from Nazareth unveiled deep things hitherto undreamed of with respect to God's ways with the world of men.

It would be only a slight exaggeration to suggest that "Father" is the one distinctly Christian word in this first Article of the Creed.[8] For when Jesus' followers praised God as "Almighty" and "Maker of heaven and earth," they were, for all the importance of these descriptions, affirming nothing radically different from what every Jew had been saying for years. But when, because of all that Jesus had said and had been, they acclaimed — and this as the thing of first importance — the Almighty Creator as the Father of Jesus Christ and their own Father, they were pointing to that uniqueness which in later years was more explicitly affirmed by the doctrine of the Incarnation: the Jesus of Galilee and Judea is also divine Son of God and as such the definitive revealer of his Father.

When one looks at the New Testament from this perspective, he is not surprised to find that it is Christocentric through and through. It was Christ who made the difference!

[8] It is for this reason that in the format of the first Article printed on page 14 we have taken the liberty of inserting commas after "God" and "Father."

II

ARTICLE TWO

PARAGRAPH 1

And in Jesus Christ,
his only Son, our Lord:

PARAGRAPH 2

Who was conceived by the Holy Ghost,
Born of the Virgin Mary:

PARAGRAPH 3

[Who for us men and for our salvation]
Suffered under Pontius Pilate,
Was crucified, dead, and buried:
He descended into hell;
The third day he rose again from the dead:
He ascended into heaven,
And sitteth on the right hand of
God the Father Almighty:
From thence he shall come to judge
the quick and the dead.

I

Introduction

The second Article proclaims Christ. And note — it is longer, as the merest glance shows, than the first and third Articles combined. The very format of the Creed illustrates that Christocentricity of the New Testament to which we pointed at the end of the last section. *Christ*-ianity is Christ![1]

Specifically, the second Article lends itself to subdivision into three natural groupings or paragraphs. The first of these preserves the titles used most frequently by Jesus' followers after his Resurrection. Each played an important role in pre-Christian Judaism. Each, too, was used by or of Jesus during the earthly ministry. As employed by believers, these titles were to all intents and purposes brief but pregnant confessions of faith.

The second paragraph recalls the circumstances of Jesus' origin. He is truly human, and yet truly divine. It is this that is proclaimed by the traditions of conception, birth, and infancy preserved for us by the Evangelists Matthew and Luke. And both statements, the Creed reminds us, affirm something absolutely essential to full understanding of what happened in Bethlehem so many years ago.

[1] The reader will recognize this as an exaggeration for emphasis. Christ was the newness which entered upon the world scene some two thousand years ago, and inasmuch as it was this which gave rise to the New Testament, he is its central theme. The doctrine of the Trinity, and the Creeds with their tripartite format (see 6 f., 15–17 above) guard against any unbalanced Christocentricity.

31

In the third paragraph the Christian recalls Jesus' suffering, death, descent into hell, Resurrection on the third day, Ascension, Session at God's right hand, and (as a sure hope) his Second Coming to the world as judge and savior at the end of time.

As an introduction to this paragraph, we have interpolated from the Nicene Creed the phrase "who for us men and for our salvation." Those events which happened in Palestine "under Pontius Pilate," that is, have a particular significance above and beyond what appears on the surface. Behind them was special point and purpose — divine purpose. Here, in other words, is *sacred* history, certain verifiable elements preserved by the tradition and by that tradition made meaningful, historical fact and theological fact, all passed on to us by those who "eye-witnessed" what actually occurred. All history is of God; but this particular bit of history, Jesus of Nazareth, was supremely and decisively so.

But all this is to presuppose something — a particular world view which was held in common by Judaism, Jesus, and then by Christianity. A "philosophical" discussion of history, an extremely complex matter, cannot be attempted here. But it is important for us to know something of the Hebraic understanding of Israel's own existence as a concrete historical phenomenon. What follows, then, is a digression, but a necessary one.

II

The Kingdom of God, the Messiah

Between the Judaism of Jesus' day and the other religions of the Mediterranean world there were significant differences. None was more striking than the contrasting concepts of deity. The Greek viewpoint considered God to be remote from the world, in many ways inscrutable. But Judaism believed that it was God's nature to reveal Himself with clarity and power.

Closely related were differing attitudes toward the world in which man lives. Hellenistic thought tended to view things material and phenomenal with a degree of suspicion. Fleshly existence, the senses, emotions were limitations to be overcome. In order to know deity and to apprehend reality (to the degree that these were possible) man must somehow rise above such encumbrances. His ultimate hope was a blessed immortality of soul loosed from the shackles of physical existence.[1]

Judaism, however, embraced *this* world. It is symptomatic that belief in a significant after-life was a relatively late phenomenon in the religion of Israel. Concrete historical realities — persons, events, every facet of life in this world — are media through which God, who is immediate Lord of history, reveals, acts, and is apprehended. Not by escape from history, but in and through history comes man's knowledge of deity. "The earth is the Lord's and the fullness thereof, the world and those who dwell therein" — and God is active throughout the entire creative process to make Himself known and to accomplish His purposes (Ps. 24:1).

The total life of the Hebrew people as recorded in the Old Testament is characterized by this view of history as immediately *of God* and *under God*. Whatever one's vantage

---

[1] Striking, however, are these words from the Wisdom of Solomon in the Apocrypha of the Old Testament: "For the corruptible body presseth down the soul, and the earthy tabernacle weigheth down the mind that museth upon many things" (9:15; A.V.). Our remarks here are significant of trends, but not to be understood as pointing to an inflexible dichotomy between Hebraic thought and that of the Mediterranean world at large. In the centuries immediately before Christ there was a considerable intermingling of Hebraic and Hellenistic thought. Such books as the Wisdom of Solomon, and others in both the canonical and apocryphal Old Testaments, evidence this fact. See further below, p. 79.

point, the past, the present, and the future were viewed in terms of what God had done, was presently doing, or would do.

We note, for example, Israel's understanding of those *past* events which constituted her as a distinctive people.

A group of Semites, living a life of virtual slavery in Egypt, sometime during the first half of the thirteenth century B.C. (*c.* 1290–1224) under the leadership of Moses left the Egyptian delta, marched through the desert wilderness to the East, and after many trials and tribulations gained a permanent foothold in Palestine. There, gradually, they succeeded in establishing themselves as a small nation.

This familiar story was handed down by word of mouth for many generations before receiving final written form hundreds of years later.[2] And the important thing is not the historical trustworthiness of every detail, but the particular interpretation given to the Exodus and ultimate settling in Palestine by those who told and re-told the story.

From the human perspective, what happened was of little significance, barely a ripple in the broad sweep of world events — which, of course, is quite beside the point. For the story was not preserved and related as something of political or international significance, but as *sacred* history. Israel looked back upon her past and recounted over and again the history of her forebears as something which *God* had done.

It was God who had called their fathers out of Egypt and led them through the wilderness. It was God who had knit together the wanderers into a community, who had made of them a people. It was God who had been with them and

[2] The narrative framework of Exodus, Leviticus, Numbers, Deuteronomy, Joshua, and Judges is concerned with the wilderness wanderings and the first struggling years in Palestine. Furthermore, in both the prophetic writings and the psalms, there is a frequent recalling of the Exodus.

through and for them conquered the land of Canaan and given it as their inheritance. It was God who had chosen them for His purposes, and in so doing had revealed to Israel — and through her to the whole world — His sovereignty, His righteousness, His will and demand for holiness, His immediate and powerful activity in His world, His tender care and love for all creation.

This tradition, as we know today, contains in its present form much that is idealized and legendary. But we do not conclude that such "non-historical" elements are unimportant. On the contrary, they are crucial to one's understanding of this history, and in this sense an essential part of it.[3] For there comes a point in man's experience when he has to resort to poetry and myth in order to say deep things which documentaries are unable to convey. So here, it is precisely the "non-literal" which is our best clue to Israel's understanding of her past as *sacred* history, her life a medium through which both the nature of God and the pattern of His relationship with the world of men were powerfully manifested.

Not only the past, however, but every *present* moment as well was viewed as immediately under God. Israel was a theocracy. She at first had no king because God was her ruler. And when finally, in imitation of surrounding states, the loose confederation of tribes adopted kingship, many opposed this innovation.

When, for example, Samuel, the last of the judges, was requested "appoint for us a king to govern us like all the nations," he acceded only because finally he was convinced that God Himself wished it. But even then the change was made with the greatest reluctance, as these words show: "for they have not rejected you [Samuel], but they have re-

[3] See above, pp. 8–10.

jected me [God] from being king over them" (I Sam. 8:4-9).
God was Israel's King! And in succeeding years this remained
the basic premise.

It was in God's name that the early prophets anointed
the nation's kings to office. Nathan's judgment against David
for his act of adultery with Bathsheba and the slaying of her
husband Uriah was meekly accepted by the king as the word
of the Lord Himself (II Sam. 12:1-15). The prophets generally were regarded as God's immediate spokesmen and
were permitted the widest latitude to rebuke and censure
Israel's sovereigns. The kings themselves were regarded as God's
vicegerents, were immediately responsible to Him, were hailed
as God's "anointed," addressed as His "Son." [4] In short, at
every present moment this tiny nation understood her history
as the immediate instrument of God's purposes.

The phenomenon of Hebrew prophecy illustrates with
special clarity this view that present historical circumstance is
no less than encounter with God Himself.[5] It was because of
this conviction that such great religious leaders as Amos, Hosea,
Isaiah, Jeremiah, and Ezekiel read contemporary events as
divine condemnation or blessing. Present difficulties of whatever kind — pestilence or famine or natural disaster or the
threat of national calamity — were proclaimed to be no less
than God's judgment against a disobedient people. At the
same time, inasmuch as God loved Israel, in repentance impelled by right understanding of present tribulation lay the
sure hope of future blessing. Thus the prophetic voice both
appealed to the conscience and promised brighter things ahead.

During the years 598-587 B.C., the nation underwent shattering experiences which included the exile of her leaders to
Babylonia. Prior to this disaster the prophets had read the
signs of the times and warned Israel's leaders to cease the

[4] I Sam. 24:6,10; II Sam. 7:14; Ps. 2:7; 45:6,7; 89:19-37.
[5] The great classical period of Hebrew prophecy began with Amos, who appeared on the scene *c.* 760 B.C., and extended over a period embracing some
two centuries.

game of power politics, to cleanse the nation from that idolatrous desire for self-aggrandizement which had led to such entanglements, lest God's condemnation strike in the guise of foreign invasion. But the warning went unheeded. The worst came, and still the prophetic voice rang out: Israel had sinned, had broken covenant; and now she must suffer divine judgment.

But it was precisely when tragedy struck that the note of hope became more insistent. Especially during the exile years, Ezekiel and the anonymous prophetic voices responsible for the last twenty-seven chapters of Isaiah bade Israel look up. God had yet a purpose for His people. The present judgment was not the end, but a purification by fire, and so a new beginning. Suffering and tribulation committed to God can re-create.

Out of present trial, then, there arose in the minds of some a deeper understanding — that the "chosen people" had been called not just for themselves, nor simply for special favor, but to be an instrument of God's continuing process of creation. Here was the deeper meaning of Israel's history. The nation would arise, be reborn, and more than this, her repentant and stubborn faith witnessing to God's power and love and forgiveness would be a "light to the nations," God's chosen people as his Servant leading all peoples to know the one true King of history.[6]

Some, we repeat, glimpsed this vision. Actually, most did not. It remained for one, Jesus of Nazareth, to live in suffering for others even to the cross, before the depth of this insight was to strike home — that the suffering of one people or of one person can alter the many, and that the pattern of all life under God is a repeated and painful dying to self in order fully to live, which is to love, which is to be the servant of others, which is the Christ life.

[6] See Is. 49:6, and generally the poems in Isaiah which describe Israel as Servant of God. See below, pp. 121-3 f.

But even so, Israel pointed the way. So vivid was the apprehension of the God who had delivered and saved and forged this people in the past, that in every given moment, in disaster no less than in joy, they sought and found His hand.

Always, too, the *future* would be God's. This aspect of Israel's faith received its most concrete expression in the years following the exile.

After the conquest of the Babylonian Empire in 539 B.C. by the Persian Cyrus, those Jewish exiles who wished were allowed to return to Palestine. Israel in a small way was reconstituted as a nation. Still, however, her life was one of privation, to a large extent dominated and oppressed by others. But contrary to what one might expect, this people's stubborn faith did not slacken. It was God who had called, God who had promised, God who loved. It was a divine purpose which was being wrought for and through Israel's existence.

More and more, then, in the midst of present difficulty Judaism spoke of future fulfillment — for Israel and for the whole world. That which God had begun, He would surely finish — in His good time. Blessing there assuredly would be. Eagerly this people looked forward to redemption.

The future, then, no less than the past and present, would mean encounter with God. And this points us to another contrast between the Hebraic and Hellenistic world views. The latter tended to think of history as cyclical. The seasons arrive, depart, return; nations rise and fall; a man is born and dies, and another takes his place. And in all this there is a recurring sameness, something without clear-cut purpose or goal.

The trend of Hebraic thinking was different. In the beginning God created the heavens and the earth, and for a specific purpose. And creation is a continuous process moving toward that divine purpose — inexorably, for God is King omnipotent. In contrast to the cyclical view, Israel's understanding of the world and life may be roughly diagrammed as an arrow. History has a beginning; history moves toward a concrete goal, *God's* End.[7]

And how was this goal depicted? The answer to this question introduces us to specific thought forms and language used both by Jesus and the first Christians. The End was termed the Kingdom of God, that is, the reign of God as King. Ultimately and surely would come the moment when He would unveil His sovereignty and with full power rule unhindered. His will which even now was being done in heaven would be done on earth as well.

The details that described the Kingdom's coming were diverse. For many, probably for most, this was a materialistic hope, the vision of an idyllic golden age *within* history, Israel triumphant over all her oppressors, Jerusalem the center of the world, economic prosperity for every son of Abraham, pain and sorrow and tears no more.

Others thought of God's End as an event which would conclude history, as something *beyond* history. This was not an aping of the Hellenistic view of "escape." For present tribulation was none the less of God, and a means of encounter with God, although more often than not a painful encounter. But lives dominated more by hardship than by joy saw the world as a battleground between an ultimately victorious God and inimical forces, and His End as requiring cataclysmic destruction and the creation of a totally new state of existence, a new heaven and earth. And the great moment, however and whenever, would be for those who persisted in opposing the fundamental fact of His kingship a terrible day of judgment. But for those able to see His hand in all, and so endure as repentant and faithful subjects, there would be perfect felicity.

None of the details, however — the oftentimes bizarre im-

[7] See below, p. 153.

agery, the materialism, the nationalistic fervor — need give us pause. Nor does the oversimplified picture which we have drawn mean that Judaism had a naïve faith in some kind of inevitable social progress which had as its center human striving. The coming of the Kingdom would be an inscrutable action of deity — man could but hope and prepare and wait. And behind it all lay the burning certainty that all creation was truly God's doing, that every circumstance is encounter with the word and action of history's Lord, and that man finds the meaning of his own existence only by accepting the divine sovereignty. God's will and purpose for the world and for Everyman are sure, and ultimately good. The Kingdom will come!

Finally, this future hope had an important corollary. As the full realization of God's sovereignty was pictured by some as an idyllic, although still earthly, kingdom, so many anticipated a human king par excellence who would rule Israel and the world as God's vicegerent. Tradition spoke of the reign of David years before (1000–962 B.C.) as the time when the tiny kingdom had reached her greatest heights. So the ideal future sovereign would be a second and even more glorious David. It is such a hope which is voiced by these familiar words: [8]

> For to us a child is born,
>> to us a son is given;
>> and the government will be upon his shoulder,

[8] Actually, Isaiah here may be referring to the new king, Hezekiah, who has just ascended his throne, and so not thinking specifically of an ideal ruler anticipated in some vague future. Nevertheless, his words, pointing as they do to what Israel desired of her kings, are a vivid expression of that ideal to which the Messianic hope was directed. The same may be said of Is. 11:2, which is quoted on pp. 161 f.

and his name will be called
"Wonderful Counselor, Mighty God,
    Everlasting Father, Prince of Peace."
Of the increase of his government and of peace
    there will be no end,
upon the throne of David, and over his kingdom,
    to establish it, and to uphold it
with justice and with righteousness
    from this time forth and for evermore.
The zeal of the Lord of hosts will do this.

(Is. 9:6,7)

In later years, Christians saw this as a prophecy fulfilled by Christ. And the Davidic hope, as it is often called, is especially important for one's understanding of the earliest Church's response of faith.

Israel's kings were anointed as a sign of their office, and, as God's chosen representatives, were hailed as His "anointed ones." It is this phrase, in Hebrew *meshiah,* which transliterated becomes our English "Messiah." In Greek, "anointed" is the adjective *christos.* And as the frustrating years passed, and the longing for another David, the perfect vicegerent of God, became stronger, Judaism began to speak of *"the* anointed one," that is, "the Messiah," or "the Christ." [9] His appearing would mean that God's Kingdom was at hand.

The Messianic hope, like the future hope of which it was a part, assumed numerous forms.[10] Some pictured Messiah as a king, others as a mighty warrior. Still another tradition anticipated a wholly supernatural figure who would come in the

[9] The first certain literary appearance of this term in a Messianic sense appears in the Psalms of Solomon, a non-canonical work written *c.* 50 B.C. This use was current in the Palestine of Jesus' day.
[10] It should be noted that while the Messiah was always understood as one intimately associated with the establishment of the Kingdom of God, not all Jews expected that there would be such a figure. Some thought of God's direct intervention and rule, without any such agent or intermediary. On the other hand, documents from the library of the sectarian group which resided at Qumran speak of two Messiahs.

41

fullness of God's time and bring the present world to its end, the "Son of Man" as he is called in the literal Greek and English renderings, meaning the particular divine agent of God's final purposes. But these and other such details need not concern us for the moment.

The importance of the "necessary digression" of the last few pages now becomes apparent. *Jesus* is the Messiah — such was the proclamation of his followers after the Resurrection. And in making this claim they were ascribing to him the most exalted status conceivable in a purely Jewish frame of reference. What they were saying, in sum, was this: the agent who brings in God's Kingdom has come; the Kingdom itself is breaking in; the divine plan which commenced with the initiation of the creative process centuries ago is about to be fulfilled; God's End, the ultimate of His will to reveal and to save, is at hand — and with untold blessing for those who truly desire that He reign.

But to hail Jesus as the Christ was, as we shall see, to say something more — that because of him, and in him, and through him, man, as never before, can discern and meet face to face and be apprehended by that which alone makes sense of his own personal history. To know him, the first Christians found, had been to have one's deepest self changed. He had not only proclaimed, he had lived his message — that God reigns, and that to accept life as His gift is to know that wholeness which is salvation. It was this, the fundamental principle of all created existence, which had shone through his life, and become a powerful reality to those who admitted their need for the divine kingship. To confess Jesus as God's Messiah was to find a personal Savior.[11]

[11] Soon, of course, the Hebraic categories of thought proved inadequate as explanation of Jesus' messiahship. Thus Christians were impelled to confess

To be sure, this was an act of faith. "I *believe* that Jesus is the Christ" — so the Creed affirms. But it was no arbitrary response. There were reasons, and to these we now turn.

III

The Christ

Names and titles are important. Long ago, "Baker," "Small," "Swift," "Miller" were so called because of actual occupations or attributes. Titles today assert something significant about an individual: "President," "Bishop," "Professor."

Or take the name "Jesus." The corresponding Hebrew word is *Joshua,* a shorter form of *Yehoshua,* and means "Yahweh saves." According to Matthew's Gospel, Joseph learned in a dream that Mary's son was to be called "Jesus, for he will *save* his people from their sins" (1:21). The Apostle Paul declared that "God has brought to Israel a *Savior,* Jesus, as he promised" (Acts 13:23). Mary's words, "and my spirit rejoices in God my *Savior,*" remind us that Judaism frequently gave this title to God (Luke 1:47). Christians have always believed that in the person and ministry of Jesus God has acted decisively to *save.*

In first-century Palestine the name "Jesus" was a commonplace in Jewish households.[1] Gradually, however, it fell into

him as divine, and the Church to evolve her doctrines of the Incarnation, and of God as Holy Trinity. One can see, however, that this later was not something totally new, but a development of the primitive confession of Jesus as Messiah. It will become even more apparent as we proceed that Christian theology "full flower" cannot be understood apart from Judaism and those Hebraic categories of thought employed by Jesus himself and the first believers.
[1] See, for example, in the New Testament, "Jesus who is called Justus" (Col. 4:11; cf. Luke 3:29).

disuse, so thoroughly had it been taken over and filled with new content by the rapidly expanding Church. On Christian lips the name had become a confession of faith and hope. That Jesus of Nazareth had been in fact "God's salvation" was precisely the thing which Judaism could not accept.

The New Testament preserves many of the titles which were used of Jesus during the early days of the Church's life. Each in its own way is "credal," a tiny confession of faith because it details something of the response which was impelled by his words and deeds and continuing presence with believers. The second Article preserves the three which were used most frequently in New Testament times. We examine each in turn.

Jesus is the Christ. Less than three full days after the arrest, trial, and execution it had all started again. Already Pilate and the Jewish religious leaders had begun to think of the whole affair as a temporary nuisance handled with dispatch. But now *this:* "You have crucified God's Messiah!" Such was the cry which resounded throughout Jerusalem. And the Gospels which preserve the Apostolic Witness to Jesus' ministry show us the "why" of this overwhelming certainty.

When Jesus came into Galilee preaching "the gospel of God," there was a stir of excitement and hope — and for two reasons. First of all, he was announcing what all longed to hear: "The time is fulfilled, and the kingdom of God is at hand" (Mark 1:14, 15). But more than this, his hearers were impressed by the authority with which he spoke and his power to perform wondrous deeds. This, too, concurred with the popular expectation. Messiah, tradition said, would be a worker of miracles. Might not Jesus be he?

The imprisoned John the Baptist, for example, relayed this question: "Are you he who is to come, or shall we look for another?" (Matt. 11:3).[2] Herod Antipas, the Jew appointed tetrarch of Galilee and Perea by the Roman government, wondered: " 'John I beheaded; but who is this about whom I hear such things?' And he sought to see him" (Luke 9:9). And there were many who asked, "Where did this man get this wisdom and these mighty works?" (Matt. 13:54).

Others were more certain. The sick, when he passed by, having heard rumors of his power to heal, hailed him as "the Holy One of God," "Son of God," "Son of David" (Mark 1:24; Matt. 8:29; 9:27; Mark 5:7). On at least one occasion, an accompanying crowd sought to "take him by force to make him king" — King Messiah (John 6:15). His entry into Jerusalem just before the passion rekindled new hopes: "Blessed be the kingdom of our father David that is coming! Hosanna in the highest!" (Mark 11:10).

Such speculation and hope were shared by the twelve closest to Jesus. Peter spoke for others as well as for himself when he impetuously burst out, "You are the Christ" (Mark 8:29). James and John were sure that he had the power to call down fire from heaven upon recalcitrant hearers, and did not hesitate to ask for special status when his Kingdom had come (Luke 9:54; Mark 10:35-40). Even Judas, some have surmised, believed him to be the Messiah until the very end, and betrayed him out of desperation, thinking thereby to force Jesus to declare himself and to act accordingly.

But something went wrong. Judas hanged himself. His ruse, if such it was, failed. By the time Jesus had arrived in Jerusalem, the first enthusiastic following had dwindled almost to nothing. At the very end, even Peter denied his earlier acclamation ("Woman, I do not know him," Luke 22:57), the remainder of the twelve hid, and only a handful, his mother,

[2] The fact that the Baptist asks this question suggests that he was not actually as certain that Jesus was the Messiah as the Matthean and Johannine traditions (for example, Matt. 3:13-17 and John 1:19-36) with respect to the baptism would lead us to believe.

two other women, and an anonymous disciple were present when he died (John 19:25-27). What had happened?

A second look at the Gospels gives the answer — a surprising one, perhaps: not only did Jesus avoid the title Messiah as a designation for himself, but his teaching and activity in general, as the crowds who at first clung to him soon found out, were a far cry from what was expected of that Son of David who was destined to return Israel to her former glory.

Repeatedly, for example, he silenced the sick who shouted his praises: "he would not permit the demons to speak, because they knew him" (Mark 1:34). He sought to suppress rumors of his mighty works: he "sternly charged them, 'See that no one knows it'" (Matt. 9:30). Asked by the religious leaders to perform miracles as a proof of Messianic commissioning from heaven, he consistently refused (Matt. 12:38, 39; 16:1-4). When the crowd sought to crown him, he "withdrew again to the hills by himself" (John 6:15). And when Peter hailed him as the "Christ," he immediately began to speak of that which was completely foreign to the current picture of the Messiah — imminent humiliation, suffering, and death (Mark 8:31; cf. 9:12 f., 31; 10:33 f.).

The evidence leaves no room for doubt. Jesus consistently tried to disassociate himself from the Messianic speculation which his ministry had caused. And it is easy to see the "why" of this, too. It was not that he spurned the Messianic hope as such, or that for which it stood. Quite the contrary. But he did reject the particular shape which it had assumed in the Palestine of his day.

The credal reference to the procurator of Judea, Pontius Pilate, recalls the contemporary scene — subjugation under Rome's yoke, heavy taxation, economic distress, constant threat to cherished traditions and patterns of worship, minor uprisings, and severe reprisals. With special and pointed eagerness many yearned for God's redemption. There were, moreover, many who felt called to take matters into their own hands, self-appointed "messiahs" such as the "Zealots" (a militant party; Simon Peter may have been a member), "Sicarii" (cloak and dagger men), abortive rebellions.[3] The air was full of rumors about "kings" and "kingdoms" — something which the Roman authorities in those tense circumstances viewed with apprehension. It sounded like threat, treason — and for the most part was.

So much, then, for the background. People knew — or at least thought they did — what kind of Messiah was needed. Jesus appeared, and announced that deliverance was at hand. The rumors flew: God has sent his Christ! Jesus tried to quell the excitement, and lost his following. Why?

For one thing, he recognized such speculation as a serious threat which might well bring his ministry to a premature end. This after all was what had happened to John the Baptist, his predecessor. True, the Gospel tradition indicates that Herodias, the wife of Herod Antipas, had a grudge against John, and that for this reason he was killed (Mark 6:14-29). But this was the least part of it. John had heralded the Kingdom, too, and attracted a following and been the subject of Messianic speculation. It was this, really, that alarmed the tetrarch who, of course, was a vassal of Roman authority. The Jewish historian Josephus put his finger on it: "Herod feared that John's so extensive influence over the people might lead to an uprising."[4] Jesus was well aware of all this. He knew, too, that there were suspicions, "Messianic talk" about himself, both in the superstitious mind of "that fox," as he once called Herod, and of many others (Luke 13:32). Some of the Pharisees (not all were uncompromisingly hostile) warned, "Get away from here [Galilee], for Herod wants to kill you" (Luke 13:31). The "Herodians," probably partisans of the tetrarch, plotted with other Pharisees against him (Mark 3:6). And what was true of Herod was true of every other Roman official in Palestine, in-

[3] Acts refers to two such uprisings under Theudas and Judas the Galilean (5:36,37).
[4] *Antiquities of the Jews*, XVIII, v. 2.

cluding Pontius Pilate in Jerusalem. This was no time to be labeled "Messiah."

Far more important, however, was another matter. The whole thrust of Jesus' message was contrary to both the temper and interests of the local scene. He was deeply concerned, and not without reason, lest the fervor of patriotic Messianism close people's ears to words which put first things first.

"Do not resist one who is evil. . . . Love your enemies and pray for those who persecute you" — was this, his hearers wondered, the way to handle the Roman oppressors (Matt. 5:39, 44)? And what of Jesus' summary of man's primary obligation with the words "love God . . . love neighbor," and the imperious manner in which he stressed and applied its inner motivation of love to every conceivable circumstance — would this free Israel from Caesar? And when challenged point-blank on *the* question of the day, who could help wondering if he cared at all about the Roman yoke: "Render to Caesar the things that are Caesar's, and to God the things that are God's" (Mark 12:13-17).

He did care, of course. But he saw things that others did not see — that external circumstances such as governments and administrations are all derivative of something more fundamental. From the first, he had determined that he must cut through the illusions of a popular Messianic hope which was dominated, and understandably so, by matters of immediate concern. "All the kingdoms of the world and the glory of them," that is, the attempt to lead his people to worldly glory and prosperity, he rejected (Matt. 4:8-10). "Man shall not live by bread alone, but by every word that proceeds from the mouth of God" (Matt. 4:4).

Not by bread *alone!* The inner stress of Jesus' preaching was no ethereal spirituality. His constant seeking out of the poor and the needy and the sick, his mighty works of healing, his entire ministry was an effective demonstration that God *is* very much concerned with the whole man in his concrete here and now. But this latter, physical and material welfare, is inseparably linked with something primary — the fact that God is King, and that man's fundamental "must" is to let *Him* reign. Until this fact is welcomed, one's life as an individual, and society as a whole will inevitably suffer. Jesus' gospel, then, was concerned not with the reversal of political fortune and·national aggrandizement, but with repentance and love.

But all this is to underline the reasons why, after their initial enthusiasm, people rejected him! After all, he had failed conspicuously to conform to the conventional expectation. True, the basic core of his gospel — God's glorious Kingdom is on the threshold — had seemed the answer to a prayer. But it didn't stand up, at least in the judgment of the hearers. Instead of threatening Rome, he had warned Israel. Instead of rallying the leaders of Judaism, he had sternly denounced them. Instead of encouraging to action, he had talked of forgiveness and love. He had not lifted one finger to meet the most critical issue of the day. Here was no leader for such times as these.

Even so, it was as King-Messiah that Jesus was condemned and executed. His efforts to disassociate himself from rumors and suspicions had failed. "We found this man perverting our nation, and forbidding us to give tribute to Caesar, and saying that he himself is Christ a king," was the witness (Luke 23:2). It was a false witness through and through, but Jesus' enemies well knew Pilate's most sensitive point.[5] And the procurator readily acceded, being subject to the same pressures as those which had forced the hand of Herod Antipas some months earlier.

On his cross was placed a superscription: "This is Jesus the King of the Jews" — one of the great ironies of history, and at

[5] According to Mark 14:62, Jesus specifically admits to being the Christ. Some scholars maintain that at the end, with nothing further to be lost, he admitted the identification in this sense: "Yes — but how blind you have been not to understand what this truly means!" However, the parallels in Matt. 26:64 and Luke 22:67–70 (cf. also Mark 15:2, Matt. 27:11, Luke 23:3), as well as Jesus' attitude in general toward the title, make this doubtful. It is the later Church's faith which shines through Mark's text.

the same time words which ever since have been the heart and core of the Christian faith (Matt. 27:37).

"Let all the house of Israel therefore know assuredly that God has made him both Lord and Christ, this Jesus whom you crucified" (Acts 2:36). This is the declaration of that same disciple, Peter, who had hailed Jesus as Messiah at Caesarea Philippi, and then given the lie to his words in the courtyard of the high priest's house. But there is no faltering now, no turning back. That which had been hoped or asserted tentatively before the Resurrection is proclaimed with absolute surety.

But how are we to understand this? After all, we have just been underlining the fact that Jesus assiduously avoided the title "Christ." Some are content to point to the Resurrection as that which impelled this proclamation. But this of itself, and for all its importance, is not sufficient cause. Between resurrection as such, and status as Messiah, there was no inevitable equation, nor even a likely one. We know that Judaism did not anticipate as deliverer one who would die and rise again.[6] Moreover, resurrection was not an unheard-of phenomenon in the folklore of the day, and certainly could be, and was, variously interpreted. There must have been something more than the appearances of the risen Jesus to induce his followers so drastically, at least on the surface, to contradict their master.

What was this "something else"? Here is an important question, because, as we have already suggested, the messiahship of Jesus is one of the foundation stones upon which the subsequent structure of Christianity was built.[7] And the answer, in brief, is this — the particular *Christian* interpretation of the

[6] The clear traces in the Gospels of initial shock and disbelief, when the news of Jesus' Resurrection first broke, underline the improbability that he himself predicted, in any such specific terms, this event. See below, p. 102.
[7] See above, pp. 42 f., fn. 11.

Resurrection (he is the Christ) *goes back to the teaching and life of Jesus himself!* For an explanation of this seeming paradox, we must turn again to the Gospel records.

It was not the future hope itself, nor Messianism as such, which Jesus rejected, but the particular posture which these had assumed in the Palestine of his day. What that posture was, we already know — a fierce nationalism, a longing for independence and revenge, material benefits. And we have already seen how strenuously Jesus sought to avoid identification with such aspirations.[8] But that which was the wellspring of Messianism, namely, the Hebraic insight that God's total sovereignty over His world is an infinitely desirable state which must and will surely be — it was this for which Jesus lived and died.[9] God's kingship, and what this means in terms of promise for the world of men, was precisely what Jesus' ministry was all about.

His followers, however, had been unable to grasp this. They had tried; and during their brief time with him, they had wondered, hoped, doubted, and hoped again. The hope is symbolized by Peter's dramatic confession: "You are the Christ" (Mark 8:29). But the inability to comprehend is equally apparent in what follows: Jesus speaks of his imminent suffering and death, and Peter "began to rebuke him" (vs. 32). The Messiah could never come to such an end. And as time drew to its close, and Jesus' adherents dwindled, and finally the last moments came, the doubts became too strong for the hopes and intimations.

But then came the shout, "God has raised him!" The details of what happened after that are less clear than one might wish. But it is not difficult to understand the impact which the

[8] See above, pp. 46–50.
[9] See above, pp. 38–40.

Resurrection caused. These, we must remember, were the same people who had been with Jesus in Galilee and Judea. Now they were joyfully and powerfully moved by the intense reality of his continued presence in their midst. They searched for the meaning of it all, and not at random, but by looking back at the earthly ministry — and with a new awareness. His true significance was something to which they had been all but blind.

But why — still we must ask — the specific conclusion that he was, after all, the Messiah? By way of anticipation, for it is this which we must detail in the next few pages, we can put it this way. Messianism had been the center of the disciples' hopes and thinking during the earthly ministry. And the Kingdom of God, with which Hebraic Messianism was inseparably linked, had been the central theme of Jesus' teaching and life. These were the categories of thought to which his adherents were accustomed, both before and during their brief association with him. Able now to formulate something of the impact which he had made, they did so in the familiar terms which they knew. They had been wrong in the kind of Messiah for whom they had looked. Nevertheless, to know him had been (and was now) to comprehend, as never before, the awesome meaningfulness of lives which fully accept God's kingship. Only the Messiah himself could have made this possible.

Specifically, now, there are three facts with respect to Jesus' earthly ministry which demanded recognition that he was the Christ.

A. Jesus heralded the imminence of God's Kingdom. This one concern dominated everything he did and everything he said.

John the Baptist had preached the same gospel. "Even now

the ax is laid to the root of the trees" (Matt. 3:10). God's "awe-full" sovereignty presses in. Jesus' submission to John's baptism was a personal affirmation of the truth of the Baptist's words. It was also the moment when he accepted as his own God-given task the burden of preparing others for the great event. And in the succeeding months (his ministry probably lasted less than a year) with an urgency hard for us to conceive — can anything be more urgent than the fact of God's dominion — he pleaded with people to listen: God wills to reign; prepare; repent!

There was for one person too little time and too much to do. He sent forth emissaries. "Carry no purse, no bag, no sandals," lest they encumber you. Do nothing, such as indulging in lengthy greetings along the road, to delay you. If one village does not listen, hasten on to the next. Hurry, before it is too late. The Kingdom comes — with threat and promise, the pearl of great price, the treasure worth every sacrifice (Luke 10:1–12; Matt. 13:44–46). "Follow me, and leave the dead to bury their own dead" (Matt. 8:22).

Nevertheless, his following dwindled. Mark's tradition tells us with surprising frankness that even some of those closest to him said, "He is beside himself" (Mark 3:21). The probability of failure and personal tragedy became clearer each day. But Jesus continued on. God wills to reign, and people must hear.

He turned his face toward Jerusalem, the holy city, the very heart of Judaism, and there spoke even more boldly and authoritatively than before. If he must suffer and die, then there was but one answer — this too was necessary to the Kingdom's coming. And on the last night he knew that such was to be the way: "I shall not drink again of the fruit of the vine until that day when I drink it new in the kingdom of God" — but the Kingdom *would* come; he and his own would share in it (Mark 14:25).

And in all this there was not one word about being himself the "Christ." And yet all his teaching, all his comings and goings, were concerned with the demand and blessing of God's sovereignty. Judaism over the years had pictured the Messiah in many different guises. But common to all was this — his work and person were to be inseparably linked with the full realization of God's reign in His world. So with Jesus.

B. Jewish Messianism, however, had another constant — the "Christ" would be the agent, the mediator of God's full kingship. Let us look again at the earthly ministry.

"But if it is by the finger (the Spirit) of God that I cast out demons, then the kingdom of God has come upon you" (Luke 11:20; Matt. 12:28). Here Jesus refers to his healings, to the indubitable fact (quite apart from the problem of the miraculous) that he was able to a remarkable degree to penetrate into people's lives. How did he understand this?

It was, he knew, not his own power, but God's which was at work here. It is the King's desire and will that man be whole, and He is powerful to accomplish that wholeness, to re-create, to save. And He was doing precisely this through those words and works of Jesus which effected not only moral change, but mental and physical health as well. Thus, the results of the earthly ministry were manifest evidence of the truth of his (Jesus') words: God's sovereignty is breaking in.

This, of course, is to understand Jesus' ministry as more than proclamation. It was instrumental. People there in Palestine actually did have their lives changed. To let God reign is not pretty sentiment, but an absolute demand, something which must be if life is to be other than mere existence. And those who admitted their need for God's kingship were, in fact, healed, made whole, saved. In the most immediate sense, the King was using Jesus' ministry to impart and to work His will for the world.

Herein lies the significance of the question asked by John the Baptist: "Are you he who is to come, or shall we look for another?" (Matt. 11:3). There is no direct answer, "Yes, I am the Christ." Jesus simply points to the observable fact that God, through him, is getting things done: "Go and tell John what you hear and see: the blind receive their sight and the lame walk, lepers are cleansed and the deaf hear, and the dead are raised up, and the poor have good news preached to them. And blessed is he who takes no offense at me" (Matt. 11:4-6). These words, significantly, are for the most part Jesus' own quotation or paraphrase of several Old Testament passages which graphically express Israel's future hope.[10] This can mean but one thing — through his mission God was actually inaugurating that for which Judaism had waited so long, the full and effectual manifestation of His kingship.

Or, to look further, note Jesus' exhortation, "Follow me." This was his frequent reply to those who were stirred by his ministry and asked what they should do.[11] The implication is clear. In some sense — and Jesus himself did not seek to define it, for his interest was not in self, but in God — his work and person were an inseparable part of that mighty action of God that he was announcing.

Of particular importance is this saying: "For whoever is ashamed of me and of my words, of him will the Son of man be ashamed when he comes in his glory and the glory of the Father and of the holy angels" (Luke 9:26). That Jesus is himself the Son of Man who is yet to come the text does not say.[12] The arrival of this heavenly figure symbolizes the moment when the coming of the Kingdom, now begun with the earthly ministry, will be complete. And here again is the integral connection between the person and work of the speaker (Jesus), and the divine End which he heralds. Whether this will be for the individual a moment of condemnation or joy will be determined by his rejection or acceptance of Jesus' words here and now.

The same stress lies behind the parable of the Last Judgment: "as you did it [or did it not] to one of the least of these my

[10] Is. 29:18,19; 35:5,6; 61:1-3. See also Luke 4:16-21.
[11] Matt. 8:22; 9:9; 19:21; Luke 9:59.
[12] See below, pp. 145-7, and particularly fn. 3.

brethren, you did it [or did it not] to me" (Matt. 25:31-46). The reference again is to Jesus' teaching. His words spell out God's demand of those who admit His sovereignty. And when the great moment comes, personal readiness and a favorable verdict at the great assize will depend upon right response to the Jesus who said, "Follow me." He is the criterion. To be his disciple is crucial.[13]

These examples must suffice. Jesus was in no sense a kingly figure. He had no thought of being so. In the end he earned a crown of thorns. But the accouterments of royalty were simply the outer garb of the current Jewish hope. Beneath, lay this — that Messiah, as vicegerent, would be an instrument of God's climactic revelation of His royal power and glory. And Jesus, without any particular thought as to personal status or office, understood his mission in these terms — his words and deeds were instrumental, used by the King to bring people to repentance, and to knowledge of what life can be when God truly is allowed to reign.

C. Finally, and most important of all, is the person of Jesus himself, and what people found there. We may perhaps put it this way. Not just in teaching or healing, but in every aspect of his earthly life, the eyewitnesses encountered what they later realized to be the burning reality of God Himself.

Jesus had said, for example, "You . . . must be perfect, as your heavenly Father is perfect" (Matt. 5:48). God is holy; and holiness is His will for man. And Jesus had lived and reflected that perfect righteousness. Here was one so empty of the wrong kind of self that he could say, "Why do you call me good? No one is good but God alone" (Mark 10:18) — and mean and live it so concentratedly that his followers could affirm that he was "one who in every respect has been tempted as we are, yet without sinning" (Heb. 4:15).[14]

"It is better for you to enter [the] life [of the kingdom]

13 See below, pp. 150-52.
14 See below, p. 66 f.

56

maimed" — with but one hand or foot or eye — "than . . . to go to hell" (Mark 9:43-48). But warnings such as this (one cannot, without consequence, disregard the commands of a holy God) were on Jesus' lips more than just proclamation. In the stern "woes" addressed to the religious leaders, in the rebukes to those who sought pre-eminence among themselves, in the cleansing of the temple which had in so many ways become a travesty of right worship — in all these, Jesus' own condemnations, there was such sure and deliberate authority that hearers knew, as never before, the "awe-fullness" and the sweeping character of divine judgment.

But the sovereign Judge is at the same time "Father," one who intimately knows His subjects, and has deep personal concern for them. It was, as we have seen, this, particularly, which Jesus stressed — and it was especially the wondrousness of personal relationship between God and man which he had made so real to those who witnessed his ministry.[15] "But even the hairs of your head are all numbered"; "do not be anxious" — about food or drink or raiment — "your heavenly Father knows that you need them all" (Matt. 10:30; 6:25-34). And he, Jesus, allowed his disciples (contrary to the law) to pluck corn on the Sabbath to allay their hunger, had carefully shown Simon and the others where they might fish with success, had known that Zacchaeus, perched upon the branches of a sycamore tree, longed to be noticed (Mark 2:23-28; Luke 5:1-11; 19:1-10). "He knew all men . . . and . . . himself knew what was in man" — this is how the fourth Evangelist expressed it (John 2:25). Here was a capacity for understanding and caring which hinted of something infinitely beyond.

"O Jerusalem, Jerusalem . . . How often would I have gathered your children together as a hen gathers her brood under her wings, and you would not" (Luke 13:34)! And seeing the city — the holy city which had nevertheless rejected God — "he wept over it" (Luke 19:41). So God yearns.

15 See above, pp. 22-5.

57

"What man of you, having a hundred sheep, if he has lost one of them, does not leave the ninety-nine in the wilderness, and go after the one which is lost, until he finds it?" (Luke 15:4). So God cares and searches for His own. And with strenuous singleness of purpose Jesus himself traveled the length of Galilee proclaiming the coming of God's salvation — traveled not only the main routes, but the byways and the back alleys too, seeking the poor and despised and unlovely. "Those who are well have no need of a physician, but those who are sick." This offended the respectable (Mark 2:15-17). But those whom Jesus found knew somehow that God did care and understand — and moreover was doing something about it.

They learned, too, that God forgives, freely, asking nothing in return but recognition of need. This was the message of the parable of the Prodigal Son (Luke 15:11-32). It was also the kind of forgiveness which the paralytic had encountered in Jesus' words, "My son, your sins are forgiven" (Mark 2:5). So also the woman taken in adultery found God's peace: "Neither do I condemn you; go, and do not sin again" (John 8:11). But there was more to this forgiveness than simply the feeling that things were right again. Somehow, to know Jesus made a difference in all kinds of ways. To hear his message of hope, to see his obvious sympathy and concern, to realize that of one's self nothing is possible, and to believe that he could help — all these things worked together to change lives. What happened was different for different people — newness of health or perspective or courage or joy to be alive. But whatever, it was because of him. He — although they learned to say this only later — was God's salvation.

To understand, to care, and to do something about it — these are personal attributes, and deeds of love. And love is at its very heart not simply an emotion, but a persistent willing of good for others and a giving of one's self, at any cost, for those others. "But I am among you as one who serves," cares, searches out, gives, loves (Luke 22:27). It was precisely and demonstrably this which Jesus' entire life, and supremely his death, had been. Such, too, is divine love, the love of God the Father for His world.

The wondrousness of God's reign is upon you! Jesus' ministry in its every aspect authenticated this message. But more than this, that earthly life had proved to be, as it were, an embodiment, an "incarnation," of that which God as King and Father is and does — so that what ultimately, because it is of a quite other realm of existence, cannot be seen, was somehow "seen." This, in the final analysis, is the "why" of the disciples' faith. Messiah it was, in the Jewish hope, through whom the ultimate of God's kingship would effect its way with the world. And to know him — Jesus of Nazareth — was for the first time, really, to know that creating, demanding, forgiving, re-creating, loving power which is the very essence of the divine King. No wonder that even before Good Friday their hearts had burned within them. And now that he was even more vividly in their midst, they understood — he was God's Christ!

Many, however, still refused to believe, including people, the Jerusalem leaders, for example, who had witnessed something of his earthly ministry. But this should not surprise us. Everything in the historical circumstances of the moment was on the side of disbelief. To all appearances, Jesus died like a common criminal. It was written in the sacred law, "Cursed be every one who hangs on a tree" (Gal. 3:13; cf. Dt. 21:23). If he had actually claimed to be King-Messiah — and many must have believed the false witness at his trial — he was obviously wrong.[16] Nor did Hebrew tradition say anything about a resurrected Messiah. Besides, only his closest followers claimed to have seen him alive.

As far as winning others was concerned, then, the first be-

[16] See above, pp. 49 f.

lievers faced a difficult task. To proclaim Jesus as the Christ was to defy all seeming. Paul probably was thinking of his own personal wrestling with this problem when he wrote, "we preach Christ crucified, a stumbling-block to Jews and folly to Gentiles" (I Cor. 1:23). And of course the principal "scandal," at least for the Jew, was the fact that Jesus' entire ministry, with the cross as climax, had been the antithesis of the popular Messianic hope of his day.

From the outset, then, there was sharp dialogue between the followers of Jesus and the adherents of Judaism. The Christian approach was essentially this: "You, as was true with us when we followed him in Galilee, do not understand what messiahship really is. You must re-read the Scriptures, search them with new understanding in the light of what has happened. Do this, and you will see that Jesus is he who fulfills them, and the hope and expectation of our forefathers."

In the pages of the New Testament there are literally hundreds of quotations or obvious paraphrases of and allusions to the text of the Old Testament. This is to say nothing of the numerous key Christian concepts ("Father," "Kingdom of God," "Messiah" are but a few of those already discussed) which have their origin in the Hebrew tradition. Here again is illustration of the "oldness" and the "newness" — Christianity as it were filled the old with new content, re-created it. And the dialogue, made inevitable by the impossible paradox (as it seemed to Judaism) of a Messiah whose throne was a cross, had a determinative influence upon the development of the earliest tradition, and continues to play this role in Christian theology.

The Church sees Christ as the climax toward which the history of Israel was pointing. It is for this reason that to understand something of this people and their literature is so necessary, if one would comprehend Christian theology and piety. At the same time, it is by knowing Christ that one can see with particular clarity the purpose and glory which were (and are!) Judaism's reason for being. And the New Testament fulfills the Old which prepares the way for it and for him to whom, actually, in different ways, both bear witness.

We today who benefit from so much new information about the Bible and the times which it reflects recognize that Christians sometimes saw things in the Old Testament which were not there. Not infrequently, for example, early believers read too much into certain texts which they claimed as prophecies of the Christian dispensation.[17] No longer do we imagine a Moses or an Isaiah as literally foreseeing the Jesus of many generations later. This, however, does not alter the picture of promise and fulfillment which was underscored above.

Jesus' own gospel was essentially that of the Hebrew Scriptures. Moreover, he himself had understood his task as the completion of the insights and hopes contained in that tradition. When, therefore, his followers claimed that Christ was the key to the Old Testament, and argued that its words pointed to him, they were carrying out a pattern which he had set and, more significant, giving voice to the reality which they had found in him. All New Testament uses of the Old Testament (including, even, the misuses) spring from the assumption that Christianity is Judaism's fulfillment, and so bear testimony to the basic conviction that Jesus is the revealing and saving action of Israel's God.[18]

We have been digressing of necessity. Because almost every

[17] Paul in I Cor. 9:8–10 provides an amusing example of this. He cites Dt. 25:4 as scriptural authority for an early custom whereby a Christian community would support a visiting church leader so that he might be entirely free for his tasks of instruction and administration: "For it is written in the law of Moses, 'You shall not muzzle an ox when it is treading out the grain.'" The Apostle goes on, "Is it for oxen that God is concerned?" No, he replies, "It was written for *our* sake," i.e., stands as divine confirmation for the support of Christian leaders by the Church. But actually, the answer is "Yes!" The Deuteronomic Code from which these words came is outstanding for its humaneness. The precise point of the text is that God *does* care for the oxen! Paul, incidentally, did not accept such support, wherever possible working with his own hands. See, for example, vss. 3–7 and 11–18.

[18] We can, then, go on to note this with respect to Paul's use of the text cited in the previous footnote — he assumes, in this passage, that the Old Testament points ahead to the new Christian dispensation, and is a divine authority even for such relatively minor matters as the particular administrative detail to which he speaks. Christianity, that is, is the goal and fulfillment of Judaism.

othei concept which we shall discuss, including the titles yet to be considered, are different ways of proclaiming this indissoluble relationship between the "old" and the "new." In Luke's Gospel there is a striking example, one given as a word of Jesus himself. The risen Lord is conversing with the two puzzled followers who were walking in despair from Jerusalem to Emmaus on the first Easter Day:

> "O foolish men, and slow of heart to believe all that the prophets have spoken! Was it not necessary that the Christ should suffer these things and enter into his glory?" And beginning with Moses and all the prophets, he interpreted to them in all the scriptures the things concerning himself (24:25–27).

The Apostle Paul in his letters uses the title "Christ" in three ways which roughly correspond to New Testament use in general.

First of all, as a Hebrew of the Hebrews, he is fully aware of the title's rich adjectival and confessional implications.[19] At one point, for example, he says of his fellow Israelites and of the Jewish patriarchs that "of their race, according to the flesh, is the Christ" (Rom. 9:5). In this passage he is commencing a long and tortuous explanation of Judaism's rejection of the claims made for Jesus. It is this same use of "Christ" which makes I Corinthians 1:23–25 such a vivid illustration of the "scandal" caused by the Christian confession: "but we preach *a Messiah crucified,* a stumbling-block to Jews . . . but . . . the power of God and the wisdom of God." [20]

On the whole, however, Paul uses this title in its full Hebraic sense relatively seldom. Much more often it appears simply as

[19] See above, pp. 40 f.
[20] We have here substituted "a Messiah" for the "Christ" in the R.S.V. See also, perhaps, Rom. 10:6 f., and I Cor. 10:4 for other examples. (Italics mine.)

the final component in such combinations as "Jesus Christ" or "Lord Jesus Christ."[21] In instances of this kind, "Christ" is to all intents and purposes a surname for Jesus. Its original connotations are far in the background, still there, if one remembers that in its origin, "Jesus Christ" meant "Jesus is the Christ," but — and this is the point — most people did not remember.

This reminds us of how early and how rapidly Christianity became predominantly a Gentile movement. Believers of non-Jewish background were less aware of the long and meaningful history which lay behind the thoroughly Hebraic title "Messiah." The result was that in common Christian parlance it soon receded into the background, becoming for most simply another name for Jesus. The fact that it was retained at all shows how firmly fixed it had been and how important, too, in the earliest tradition.

But Paul repeatedly uses the title in a third way. He reverses the order of the two "names," and the result is such phrases as these: "baptized into Christ Jesus"; "alive to God in Christ Jesus"; "those who are in Christ Jesus"; "in Christ Jesus . . . through faith" (Rom. 6:3,11; 8:1; Gal. 3:26). This practice is peculiar to the Apostle, and represents one of his unique contributions to Christian tradition.[22]

In Greek syntax, to place "Christ" first is to give it special emphasis: The *Christ* is he! Perhaps in this manner Paul was attempting to rescue the title from its "back seat" role in Gentile Christianity. Be this as it may, he does give to the title a new dimension of meaning. For it would seem significant that the order "Christ Jesus" is employed (as in the examples above) with special frequency in contexts which underline the relationship between believers and their risen Lord. The same title standing by itself is often used in like fashion: Christ lives

---

[21] See, for example, the benedictions and blessings cited above, pp. 25 f.
[22] Aside from a few scattered instances in Acts, and apart from those letters which are almost certainly Paul's, we find this reversal of order only in Ephesians, I, II Timothy, and Titus. Those who conclude that these are pseudonymous letters cite such uses as imitation of Paul's style.

in the Christian, or the believer lives "in Christ" — the heavenly exalted one, for "even though we have known Christ after the flesh, yet now we know him so no more" (II Cor. 5:16; A.S.V.).[23] The Apostle, in short, has underlined the primitive Messianic confession as something far more than simply an intellectual assent to a fact. To know Jesus as the Messiah is to live the "Messiah life," which is the "in Christ" life. In this manner Paul points to the ultimate of Christian experience as a deeply personal union of the believer with a personal Savior.[24]

This is an especially clear example of the "newness" which is Christianity. Jesus had penetrated to the heart of Judaism's future and Messianic hope. His followers in hailing him as Messiah had been faced with the necessity of changing their own comprehension of what Messianism meant. Paul's concept of life "in Christ" helped immeasurably to spell out the new Christian understanding of the traditional Jewish concept. As a result, the title was, as it were, re-created, filled with a new content, and thereby became deeply significant for the piety of all Christians. To be "in Christ" was to heed Jesus' injunction, "Follow me."

IV

God's Son, Our Lord

Jesus the Christ is *divine* Son of God and Lord. The Apostolic Witness so confessed him, long before the time of the later Trinitarian Creeds. Here we must examine a different dimension of the early faith, one which goes far beyond the bound-

[23] See, for example, I Cor. 1:2; II Cor. 1:21; 5:17; Gal. 2:20.
[24] See below, pp. 185–7.

aries of Judaism. The concept of messiahship, for all its richness, proved inadequate to explain and express the startling newness which had upturned the lives of Jesus' followers. At a very early date, believers — Jewish Christians as well as converts from the Gentile world — began to worship Jesus as a divine being, and accorded him a status and function approximating that of God Himself.

The "how" and the "why" of this transition is the concern of the next few pages. We shall use the titles Lord and Son of God as our chief examples.

Frequently, the Gospels tell us, the earthly Jesus was addressed as "Lord." Consider the following texts:

> Lord, if you will, you can make me clean (Matt. 8:2).

> Lord, how often shall my brother sin against me, and I forgive him? (Matt. 18:21).

> Master, it is well that we are here (Mark 9:5).

> Good teacher, what must I do to inherit eternal life? (Mark 10:17).

"Lord" in the first two passages is a translation of the Greek *Kyrios*. Still further behind this lies the Aramaic which was spoken in the Palestine of the time. Thus the actual word on the lips of Jesus and his contemporaries was *Mar*.[1]

This word was a common title of respect used by slaves of their masters, or pupils of their teachers. It meant much the same as "Sir" does today. Jesus himself used *Mar* in this sense. In the parable of the Wheat and Tares the servants say to the householder, "*Sir,* did you not sow good seed in your field?" (Matt. 13:27). Or Jesus says, "A disciple is not above his

---

[1] In these examples, we cite the nominative case, rather than the vocative.

teacher, nor a servant above his *master*" (Matt. 10:24). In each instance the italicized word is a rendering of *Mar, Kyrios*.

So the prophet from Nazareth, who awed many with his mighty works, and with his authoritative and knowledgeable manner of teaching, was addressed with respect, and even by those who opposed him: "Teacher," "Master," "Sir." And the few — the very few — who stayed with him until the final hours tendered him such loyalty and obedience as their limited understanding of the moment allowed.

When we today read "Lord" in the Gospels, it is "divine Lord" which rings in our minds. This doubtless is what the Evangelists, writing as believing Christians in the late decades of the first century, intended. For so they knew him to be. But during the earthly ministry Jesus was not worshiped as divine.[2]

The immediate background of the title Son of God is Jesus' own use of the language of filial relationship. This idiom, as we saw, reflects his personal total obedience and dependence upon God.[3] This sonship was not for him an object of speculation or of theological concern — it simply was. We shall consider a bit later the process whereby Christians came to confess Jesus as *divine* Son. But this, as well as the formal doctrines of Incarnation and Holy Trinity, have their origin in observable facts with respect to the earthly ministry. At this point, let us cite one example.

To a questioner who addressed him as "good teacher," Jesus replied, "Why do you call me good? No one is good but God alone" (Mark 10:17,18). Some find this an acute embarrassment to Christian faith in the divinity of Jesus. Quite the contrary, however; it points to important aspects of Jesus' earthly life

---

[2] Doubtless people considered him, as a miracle worker, to possess supernatural powers; but this is a very different matter.

[3] See above, pp. 23–5.

which elicited this confession. The words just quoted from Mark's Gospel express complete self-abnegation. They underscore that striking dependence upon God which prompted Jesus' use of the concepts of sonship and fatherhood. Only one totally devoid of that wrong kind of self which stands against God could speak in this way, and so obviously mean it — obviously, because it was apparent to those who knew him in the flesh that even to the final moment of giving on the cross, every concern and every effort was for others. There was another observable phenomenon, too, the healings. His words and works did in fact change people's lives.

Perfect obedience to God and, because there was no barrier of self, freedom unreservedly to give to others — this, then, was the Jesus whom the eyewitnesses knew. Free of self, he was found to be (admittedly, this is crude and untheological) "full of God." For no less before the cross than after he had proved to be a channel of God's concern and power to forgive, to re-create, to sustain, to love.

The Apostolic Witness, then, points to a life which was the "incarnation" of what God wills for man and what God does for man. It was this recognition with respect to Jesus' humanity which elicited the realization that he was more than one among many brethren — the divine Son of God, the visible expression of the invisible God, the Savior sent by God.[4]

Jesus' Resurrection had settled one question in the minds of

[4] Some of the Gospel miracle stories, which otherwise seem to many today hard to understand, become especially meaningful when seen in this light. Jesus, for example, calms a storm, walks on water, changes water into wine. Whether or not he actually did wonders of this kind is far less important than the deep underlying truth which prompted early Christians to tell and retell such stories — the personal experience, based upon encounter with the crucified-risen one, that to confess Jesus as the Christ is to know the sustaining power of God Himself. Such stories, then, are an important part of the Apostolic Witness. See above, pp. 8–10.

his followers. He was far more than a teacher or prophet. That sonship of which he himself spoke was a very special kind. Messiah had come! But still they asked, "Who is he? What, indeed, has God done here?" — for they found themselves to be laid hold of by something which far exceeded earlier expectations or hopes.

In the search for an answer, the titles Son and Lord played an important role, partly because they had already been used in connection with the earthly ministry, and because, too, believers found precedent in the Old Testament which made these words especially meaningful. In brief, Christians began to use these titles as alternate ways of proclaiming Jesus' messiahship and its meaning. The following Old Testament passages introduce us to the "why" and the "how" of this first step:

> I will tell of the decree of the Lord:
> He said to me, "You are my son,
>   today I have begotten you" (Ps. 2:7).

> The Lord says to my lord:
> "Sit at my right hand,
> till I make your enemies
>   your footstool" (Ps. 110:1).

Both of the psalms which we cite here had in the past been used as paeans of praise in connection with the enthronement of Jewish kings. These rulers, we remember, were considered to be the representatives of God, the true King. We may, then, paraphrase as follows:

> [God] said to me [the king], "You are
>   my son, today I have begotten you."
> The Lord [God] says to my lord [the
>   king]: "Sit at my right hand . . ."

In such manner, then, were underlined both the special relationship (sonship) between the monarch and God, and the king's role as authoritative vicegerent (lordship in the place of special honor at God's right hand) of the theocratic kingdom's true Sovereign.

In all probability, pre-Christian Judaism did not stress these texts as Messianic prophecies. Both psalms, however, in Jesus' day were used by worshipers in temple and synagogue. And to Jesus' followers their true meaning seemed obvious.[5] Had he not spoken repeatedly of God as his Father? Had he not sought to explain the significance of his baptism at the hands of John in terms of consecration to special sonship (Mark 1:9-11)? Had he not himself in debate with the Jerusalem leaders suggested that "Lord" was a far more appropriate title than "Son of David" for the Messiah (Mark 12:35-37)? [6] Had not his words been so authoritative as to amaze his hearers, and so charged with power as to upturn lives? And was not he — he whom they had followed, however imperfectly, as Lord and Master during the earthly ministry — as the risen one more meaningfully and powerfully the dominant factor of their own existence than even before his Crucifixion?

To the early Christians, the evidence was indisputable. His own words, his own life of obedience and powerful sonship, corresponded to the words of these psalms. His Resurrection, of course, meant that he was now enthroned at God's right hand. All this was proof, and the psalms were a divine foretelling, that Jesus was the Messiah, and that he who had been their Lord before Good Friday was still their Lord now in heaven.

[5] The importance of these two psalms to the early Church can be seen from the frequency with which they are quoted by the New Testament tradition. Ps. 2:7 appears at least five times, and Ps. 110:1 at least fifteen times. This is to say nothing of other probable allusions, and the fact that other parts of these same Psalms are also quoted.
[6] There is some question about this passage as an authentic saying of Jesus, but if actually reflecting Jesus' own view, it shows that he interpreted Ps. 110:1 as Messianic prophecy. He does not, it should be noted, identify himself with the Messiah of whom he speaks. See below, p. 133.

The earliest post-Resurrection use of these two titles, then, underlined and detailed Jesus' messiahship. To term him Son was to point to the Christ as one so closely connected with God as to be a unique and authoritative expression of the divine will and purpose and way. To hail him as Lord was to say that he continued to be the object of their loyalty and obedience — only now more so than ever — and the authority over their own lives. In this first stage, primitive Christians were not affirming Jesus' divinity, by which we mean that he shares in the essential attributes of deity. But to confess him as Messiah was to avow that what happened "under Pontius Pilate" was an unparalleled action of God Himself.

We have been describing the earliest groping attempts at a Christology ("word about Christ"). How different, now, the idiom and tone of these Pauline texts:

1. yet for us there is one God, the Father, from whom are all things and for whom we exist, and one Lord, Jesus Christ, through whom are all things and through whom we exist (I Cor. 8:6).

2. And whatever you do, in word or deed, do everything in the name of the Lord Jesus, giving thanks to God the Father through him (Col. 3:17).

3. who, though he was in the form of God, did not count equality with God a thing to be grasped . . . Therefore God has highly exalted him . . . that at the name of Jesus every knee should bow . . . and every tongue confess that Jesus Christ is Lord, to the glory of God the Father (Phil. 2:6–11).

4. But when the time had fully come, God sent forth his Son, born of a woman, born under the law, to redeem those who were under the law (Gal. 4:4).

These are key texts, and representative of many others. We cannot stop to do them justice. Briefly, the titles Son of God and Lord are no longer simply other ways of hailing Jesus as the Messiah of Judaism. He is divine Son and divine Lord.[7] Paul's Christology includes these three points:

a. Jesus the Christ is one who pre-existed in heaven before descending to earth for man's salvation (Nos. 1, 3, 4).

b. There is an undefined equality of status and function between God and Christ (Nos. 1, 3). Many Pauline texts evidence this same parallelism, notably the benedictions and blessings discussed on pages 25–8 f. above.

c. Christ is the object of cultic worship; to him and through him are praise and intercession made (Nos. 2, 3).

All this is to move well beyond the boundaries of normative monotheistic Judaism. In the past, to be sure, the expected Messiah had been depicted in glowing terms, in some circles, even, regarded as a pre-existent heavenly being with supernatural powers. But the whole tendency of the Apostle's words, pointing as it does, however imprecisely, to equality, is a very different thing indeed. The Jewish Messiah was anticipated with awe as instrumental to God's ultimate Self-revelation and blessing. But worship through and of Jesus as divine Lord of the Christian cultus goes well beyond this.

Proclamation of Jesus' divinity came to the fore very early. Paul's letters, for example — those at least indubitably his — reflect Christian thinking of the sixth decade.[8] And clearly his exalted Christology represents nothing novel at that time, either to his readers or to himself. He does not defend or argue, but simply assumes the Messiah's divine status. Moreover, many of

[7] The development of Christian use of these titles and concepts was not as neatly schematic as we, for purposes of organization and clarity, make it appear. It would be more accurate to speak of predominant trends, and these in many cases must have been parallel rather than successive.
[8] See Appendix I.

the texts which reflect this "high" Christology are themselves words that he quotes or paraphrases. We have at least three of these among our own examples on page 70 above (Nos. 1, 2, 3), actual fragments of very early Christian liturgy and hymnology. Paul, in other words, was following an already well-established habit pattern. In short, everything points to confession and worship of Christ as divine as something which became explicit during the very first generation of the Church's life.

This is not to suggest that there was immediately created a full-fledged systematic theology to which all promptly acceded. Far from it. For some, a simple adoptionist Christology — the view that Jesus had been rewarded for his goodness by being raised from the dead and given the prize of messiahship — sufficed.[9] Others, at least for a time, probably remained content with a simple Jewish Messianism. Worship of Jesus as divine represents yet another perspective. Nor with respect to this last had the earliest Christians thought through all the implications of their confession.

Frequently, for example, and often in the same contexts where he sets God and Christ side by side in a parallelism of status and function, Paul nevertheless subordinates the Son. In the familiar Philippians hymn, for example, Jesus is first mentioned as he who "though he was in the form of God, did not count equality with God a thing to be grasped." But at the end of this same passage, confession of Jesus' Lordship is "to the [sole] glory of God the Father" (Phil. 2:6, 11). In the benedictions, "grace . . . and peace" are equally "from God our Father and the Lord Jesus Christ." [10] In I Corinthians 8:6 (cited on page 70 above) the parallelism between God and Christ is striking. Later, however, in the same letter the Apostle writes, "When all things are subjected to him [Christ], then the Son himself will also be subjected to him who put all

[9] See, for example, Acts 2:36.
[10] See above, p. 70.

things under him, that God may be everything to every one"
(I Cor. 15:28).

Such inconsistencies are hardly surprising. The Apostolic
Witness contains many such, and with respect to numerous
areas of Christian thinking. Formal theology was still in the
process of becoming long after the books of the New Testament had been written. Considerably before Paul took pen in
hand, many had come to know and to worship Christ as divine,
assumed and were perfectly at home with this idiom. But consistent and systematic "theologizing" had barely begun.

The "how" of this transition is important, too. It illustrates
with special clarity that dialogue between the earliest Church
and the world at large which was essential, if Christianity was
to realize its potential as a universal religion.

In a Church that was rapidly coming to be dominated by
Gentiles, Son of God and Lord soon became the primary confessions of faith. One reason for this is the fact that both titles
were current in the pre-Christian religions from which these
converts had been won.

For centuries devotees had spoken of their legendary saviors,
cult deities, idols, as divine "sons of God" and divine "lords."
The Mediterranean world abounded with cults centering upon
dying and rising deities who held forth the promise of blissful
immortality. Often, too, kings and emperors were "worshiped"
and hailed as divine. The importance and meaningfulness of
the confession *Kyrios Iēsous* (Jesus is Lord) is underlined by
its counterpart *Kyrios Kaisar* (Caesar is Lord) (Rom. 10:9;
Phil. 2:11). And many a Christian in early times was ordered
to swear his civic loyalty by proclaiming "Caesar is Lord" and
anathema Iēsous, that is, "cursed be Jesus" (I Cor. 12:3).

When, therefore, early converts from a Gentile background
found that their predecessors in the faith were using Son of

God and Lord, they welcomed these titles as something familiar. As we have seen, the context of this earliest Christian use differed from that of pagan Gentile practice. For one thing, the titles were rooted in Jewish Messianism. Moreover, they centered not upon a legendary figure, but upon a real person, Jesus of Nazareth. But these two differences lead us directly to the point. Messianic categories of expression, for all their richness, were rapidly proving inadequate as explanations of all that was happening in the lives of believers. Gentile converts from their own background brought to "Son" and "Lord" a new dimension of understanding, that of divine status. At the same time, the fact that it was the *historical* Jesus who was so designated gave to the concept of divinity a concreteness and a meaningfulness undreamed-of by any Gentile before his conversion to Christianity.

But there was another closely related phenomenon which contributed to the transition. In the Greek Old Testament, the term most frequently used to translate the chief Hebrew word for God (*Yahweh*) was *Kyrios,* "Lord." [11] The familiar Psalm 110:1 affords an excellent example. In the Greek translation, the words for God and His vicegerent are identical: "The Kyrios [God] says to my kyrios [the earthly king]: 'Sit at my right hand. . . .'" Christians, of course, saw this as a reference to their King Messiah.[12] So we have the phenomenon, using now the English translation, of both God and Messiah-Jesus being designated as "Lord." Or take the words of Joel 2:32: "all who call upon the name of the Lord shall be delivered." Here too, "Lord" refers to God, and in the Greek version appears as *Kyrios.* And Paul, quoting these same words

[11] This Greek version, called the "Septuagint" (commonly abbreviated LXX), was gradually produced by different translators over a period of many years, and was complete, except for a few books not found in the canonical Old Testament, by the end of the second century B.C. The chief factor leading to this translation was the need of Greek-speaking Jews who lived outside Palestine, and were more familiar with Greek than with Hebrew and Aramaic. The LXX became the Bible of most Gentile Christians.

[12] See above, pp. 67–70.

in Romans 10:13, takes "Lord" as a reference to Jesus whom Christians now confess as "Lord" (vs. 9).

There is no doubt that this linguistic phenomenon had an important effect. Greek-speaking believers found the word "Lord" being used for Jesus in the Christian cultus and also, in the Old Testament, for God. This inevitably suggested some kind of identity between Jesus and God (that this was an "uncritical" view would not occur to most in that day), and was a further factor leading the Church to hail her Lord as divine.

To recognize such factors as verbal parallelisms and mere surface similarities of usage in Jewish, Christian, and pagan religious praxes is to realize that fortuitous circumstance played a role at a crucial stage in the development of early Christology. But this is something that may be welcomed as illustrative of a basic premise of the Church's faith — that God does indeed use history as a medium of His purposes. And this means that He uses not simply that which is on the grand scale, sweeping movements and dynamic events, but equally the ordinary "stuff" of history, all the things that make life what it is — geographical circumstances, cultural circumstances, real persons, their ignorances no less than their talents, their needs equally with their insights and strengths, in short, everything. So what seems to be fortuitous circumstance, and from one perspective is, has deep meaning when viewed "under God."

Beyond this, however, is that one particular constant to which every page of the New Testament witnesses — the dynamic of an event so impelling that even today it keeps spilling out over the boundaries of human attempts to explain or define. On the surface it may seem as if it were largely chance which led to this new Christological development. But actually and ultimately, it was Christian experience, the overwhelming and powerful newness, that is, of lives which accepted Jesus as the Christ, which constrained believers to worship him as divine. In brief, the Church was in need of and ready for this step. Only by taking it were Paul and his contemporaries able to make sense out of what had happened to them — all because of God's Messiah. The divinity of Jesus is, and remains, a confession of faith. But behind it, there lies a reading of those things that happened "under Pontius Pilate" which was in no sense arbitrary.

V

Only

This single adjective is important out of all proportion to its brevity. It introduces us to the most exalted Christology to which the early Church attained in New Testament times.

In the first days, there was no need to stress the obvious — that Messiah Jesus was unparalleled event. Pre-Christian Judaism anticipated the new age as climactic and decisive. And the coming of Jesus had proved to be precisely this in the experience of the first Christians. Thus it was not until later that there was specific and conscious theological underlining of the uniqueness of Christ.[1] So the Fourth Gospel speaks of him as "the *only* Son from the Father" (1:14). From the same pen come these familiar words: "For God so loved the world that he gave his *only* Son . . ." (3:16; cf. I John 4:9; italics mine).

Special circumstances made this underlining necessary. In the earliest days, for example, the words "son" and "sonship" were often used to characterize Christian believers. The Apostle writes in reference to his readers' baptism: "For all who are led by the Spirit of God are *sons* of God. For you did not

[1] The tradition of Jesus' birth of a virgin, of course, stresses his uniqueness. See below, pp. 85–96.

76

receive the spirit of slavery to fall back into fear, but you have received the spirit of *sonship*" (Rom. 8:14, 15; cf. Gal. 4:4–7; italics mine). The Greek word for "son" here, *huios,* is the same as that used for Jesus as the "Son" of God. In the later Fourth Gospel, and in the Johannine Epistles, significantly, "son" is never used of believers who are instead designated as *tekna* (children), and "Son" is reserved solely for Jesus. In this manner the latter's uniqueness is made perfectly clear. To become a Christian is not to become divine.

But there was another contributing factor. In the Gentile world there were many "lords" and "sons of God." Paul takes note of this in words which we have already quoted: "For although there may be so-called gods . . . and many 'lords' — yet for us there is one God . . . and one Lord, Jesus Christ . . ." (I Cor. 8:5, 6). The Son of God whom the Christian knows is something utterly new.

Far more important, however, is the fact that the adjective "only" points us to Logos Christology. For it is this latter which in New Testament times most clearly detailed in theological terms the uniqueness of Jesus as the Christ. Here too is the immediate biblical background for the lengthy setting forth of Jesus as the "only begotten Son" in the Nicene Creed.

"Logos" is the Greek term for "word." And a "word," whether written or spoken, is something intelligible. It conveys meaning because it is a product of logical (from the Greek "logos"!) thought, and is addressed to one capable of logical thought. It is because of this that the same term "logos," is used in Greek parlance to signify man's power of comprehending and ordering what he comprehends, namely, "reason."

In both Hebraic and Hellenistic religious vocabularies, the term "logos" played a significant role. Both Jew and Gentile, each in his own way, believed deity to be self-revealing, knowable by a dependent creation. And both conceived of the divine Word as the medium of such activity and Self-disclosure.[2]

In the Hebrew tradition, for example, God's Word is creative: "In the beginning . . . God *said,* 'Let there be light . . . Let there be a firmament' . . . And it was so" (Gen. 1:1–31; cf. Ps. 33:6; 148:8). Or God speaks through the prophets ("Thus *says* the Lord," "Hear the word of the Lord"), and the meaning of contemporary events in terms of threat and promise is revealed.[3] Or God as righteous speaks his will for holiness, both through the prophets, and also through the Torah, which is divine law, written and oral. And all these words are God's Word, and not only reveal, but as divine command get things done. The following passage is an illuminating expression of this latter:

> For as the rain and the snow come down from heaven,
>> and return not thither but water the earth,
> making it bring forth and sprout,
>> giving seed to the sower and bread to the eater,
> so shall my word be that goes forth from my mouth;
>> it shall not return to me empty,
> but it shall accomplish that which I purpose,
>> and prosper in the thing for which I sent it
>
>> (Is. 55:10 f.).

In brief, God's Word, as the intelligible instrument which reveals and effects, is the way of His relationship with His world.

In Greek thought, too, the Logos or Word was viewed as a means of divine activity. Many at the time of Christian origins conceived of that outward thrust of deity which creates and sustains the universe as an emanation from God, itself divine. As agent of God, this emanation was regarded as a separate entity and sometimes personified, and called the Word because deity can be known. Thus the Logos was revealer,

[2] This is not to ignore the sharp differences which we noted above, pp. 32 f., 38 f.
[3] This has been discussed above, pp. 36–8. See Is. 1:10, 10:24, 43:14, etc.

agent of creation, giver of light and life, Savior. For the knowledge which can be apprehended through the Logos is knowledge of deity; and to know God, His way with and for the world, alone makes possible truly meaningful existence.

For all their differences, Judaism and Hellenism had, in this concept of the divine Word, something in common. And we have evidence that this was recognized in the centuries immediately before Christ. In the later books of the Old Testament, and in some of the Apocryphal writings, for example, Torah (Law) and Wisdom are spoken of as semi-personified divine entities, of God, and yet separate and instrumental in the creation of the universe and in the giving and sustaining of life.[4] Many Jews, such as Philo Judeus, a contemporary of Jesus, had come to admire the insights of Hellenistic religious philosophy, and sought to interpret the Hebraic tradition in their light.[5] All in all, this phenomenon of "Hellenistic Judaism" represents an important background for Christian understanding of the Messiah as unique divine event, and supplied categories of thought which were crucial for later theological thinking.

It is in this context, as outlined above, that the meaning of passages such as these becomes clear:

> yet for us there is one God, the Father, from whom are all things and for whom we exist, and one Lord, Jesus Christ, through whom are all things and through whom we exist (I Cor. 8:6).

> He [Christ] is the image of the invisible God, the first-born of all creation; for in him all things were created, in heaven and on earth, visible and invisible. . . — all things were created through him and for him. He is before all things, and in him all things hold together (Col. 1:15-17).

> In many and various ways God spoke of old to our fathers

[4] See, for example, Prov. 8:22-31, Wisd. Sol. 7:22 — 8:1, etc.
[5] Philo was born c. 20 B.C., and died c. A.D. 45. His voluminous writings are the chief extant extra-biblical evidence of "Hellenistic Judaism."

by the prophets; but in these last days he has spoken to us by a Son, whom he appointed the heir of all things, through whom also he created the world. He reflects the glory of God and bears the very stamp of his nature, upholding the universe by his word of power. When he had made purification for sins, he sat down at the right hand of the Majesty on high, having become as much superior to angels as the name he has obtained is more excellent than theirs (Heb. 1:1-4).

In the beginning was the Word, and the Word was with God, and the Word was God. He was in the beginning with God; all things were made through him, and without him was not anything made that was made. In him was life, and the life was the light of men. . . . And the Word became flesh and dwelt among us, full of grace and truth; we have beheld his glory, glory as of the only Son from the Father (John 1:1-4, 14).

Only in the last of these is Word (Logos) specifically mentioned. Elsewhere in the New Testament it occurs as a title only in I John 1:1, and Revelation 19:13. In Hellenistic religions and philosophy the concept had many associations, some impossible to reconcile with the Christian gospel. The term therefore, was initially used with a certain reticence, and really came into its own later than New Testament times. Nevertheless, it is a Logos Christology in rudimentary form which is reflected in all the texts cited above. The first two, incidentally, as words of Paul, indicate that both he and other Christians were conversant with this manner of thinking long before it became (as in the Fourth Gospel) the subject of conscious and schematic theologizing.

It is a pre-existent "cosmic" Christ whom these texts confess.[6] By this we do not mean that Jesus of Nazareth, prior to his earthly life, existed as a recognizably human but heavenly

---

[6] Technically, perhaps, one ought to use the term "Christ," or "Jesus Christ," only for the crucified-risen one, that is, for the divine Logos as *incarnate*. It is the divine Word which pre-exists, not Jesus Christ.

figure in the skies. What we are saying, however, is that Jesus the Christ is here proclaimed as the key to man's knowledge and understanding of the total created cosmos and its relationship to God its Creator — because to confess Jesus as the divine Logos is to know him as the manifestation on the plain of history of that divine Word through which God creates, reveals, acts. Note in this connection the functions of Christ in the texts cited above:

1. agent or intermediary of the initiatory creative process: "through whom are all things" (I Cor.); "in him all things were created . . ." (Col.); "through whom also [God] created the world" (Heb.); "all things were made through him, and without him was not anything made that was made" (John).

2. agent or intermediary of the sustaining process: "through whom we exist" (I Cor.); "in him all things hold together" (Col.); "upholding the universe by his word of power" (Heb.); "In him was life, and the life was the light of men" (John).

3. the goal, the fulfillment of the universe, that toward which the total creative process is headed: "all things were created . . . for him" (Col.); "whom [God] appointed the heir of all things" (Heb.).

In brief, Christ is all in all, the beginning, the end (God's End!), and all that intervenes. Around him the entire universe revolves. From him it takes its meaning.[7]

The followers of Jesus had witnessed and experienced an historical event which had come to dominate every aspect of their lives — and this in a manner and to a degree hitherto undreamed-of. How were they to understand this? It was through His Word — which as Word of command is powerful to initiate and to bring to completion, and as intelligible Word reveals and can be known — that God creates, gives

[7] Such a proclamation clearly obviates any need for a *new* "space theology."

and sustains life, delivers, re-creates, brings all existence and history to their fulfillment. And it was only by confessing Jesus Christ as that divine Word now made manifest within history — for everything that they had become and were they knew to be because of him — that believers were able, at all adequately, to understand and explain the new creation of their own lives. This was what messiahship meant.

Logos Christology was a medium of expression potentially meaningful to hearers and converts from both Jewish and Gentile backgrounds. Its possibility for subsequent theological development was, as succeeding centuries have shown, especially rich. It was one of those necessary bridges which enabled the Church to recognize that hers was a universal gospel. Here at last was a way of saying, as adequately perhaps as one ever can, that the key to all that man would know or need know about the world and his own part therein is to be found in this one historical event which occurred almost two thousand years ago. In confession of him as the divine Word, the Apostolic Witness to the inexhaustible significance of Jesus Christ as unique event of God reaches its climax.[8]

The Christian says that if any man would see and know the invisible God, he has but to look at Jesus Christ. Such, stated in untheological terms, is the doctrine of the Incarnation. The divine Logos became incarnate, that is, was at a particular point of history "en-fleshed," "en-manned."

This cardinal tenet has its origin in the witness of those who companied with Jesus during the earthly ministry. Looking back, his followers knew that they had actually encountered in him, and face to face, that ultimate reality which he had proclaimed.[9] It could not be otherwise; for everything that

[8] See further below, pp. 135-7.
[9] See above, pp. 56-9.

he said and did and was before Good Friday proved afterwards to be even more creative of new lives. God had in a most immediate sense visited and redeemed them and all his people.

It has over the years proved impossible to explain with full adequacy the "how" of the one Jesus' true humanity and true divinity. But the New Testament Church tried, and not ineffectually, either. We must look again at the texts cited on pages 79f.

In both Colossians and Hebrews, Jesus bears the relational title, Son. He is further described — and the two are different ways of saying much the same thing — as "the image of the invisible God," and as one who "reflects the glory of God and bears the very stamp of his nature" (Col. 1:15; Heb. 1:3). Such words as these go well beyond that vague undefined kind of equality of status and function which we noted in connection with other texts.[10] Now we have affirmations compelled by the certainty that Jesus is the Reality of God Himself. The phrases are conscious attempts to define that relationship with some precision.

An ideally perfect image reproduces the real thing with detailed exactitude. So, too, with the perfect mirror: Jesus Christ "reflects" God's glory. And from the stamp or seal the soft wax receives an impression which is indubitably recognizable.

Nor is this just a superficial or surface representation of deity. The Son is, to use another possible translation for the verb "reflects," the "effulgence" of God's glory. That is, as light radiates from, and yet is, the real thing, and as the divine Logos emanates from God, so between Jesus Christ as the Logos incarnate, and God, there is identity of essence or being. Nor is there anything partial or incomplete about this divine Self-revelation. "Glory" in the Hebraic idiom bespeaks deity in all the fullness of His sovereign majesty and splendor. It

[10] See above, pp. 70–3.

is this which Jesus Christ makes manifest: "For in him dwells the whole fullness of deity bodily" (Col. 2:9; cf. 1:19). And he is the image of God's very inmost being. This is the meaning of the word "nature," which may also be rendered "substance," or "reality."

Admittedly the language is inadequate to the task. The fact that all three — the image, the mirror, the stamp — are lifeless representations of the original is simply a reminder that there is no such thing as a perfect analogy, and particularly here where the attempt is to express with finite language that which is Infinite. But the intent and the conviction of the writers are clear. Jesus Christ, no less before than after the Crucifixion, was the manifestation of the eternal Word of God. So truly and so completely was that Word identified with our human circumstance, that in every aspect of that particular human life, man discerns all that God is and does in relationship with His world.

The passage cited from the Fourth Gospel is most explicit of all. In the opening verses, without specific reference to Jesus, the divine Logos is described in the terms which we have already noted — his pre-existence as an entity separate from God, his identity of being with God, his agency in the creative process, his role as life giver and sustainer.

Then in verse 14 that towards which the writer has been moving is made explicit. The *earthly* Jesus is that divine Logos: "So the Word became flesh; he came to dwell among us, and we saw his glory" (N.E.B.). And this "glory" is no less than God's glory — "such glory as befits the Father's only Son." Thus, not in some mythical deity of prehistoric times, nor in some spiritual apparation, but in one who has in every way shared our own human circumstance is God to be discerned. "What God was, the Word was" — so the New English Bible aptly renders John 1:1. But the Word became fully identified with Jesus of Nazareth: what the Word was, Jesus was. Through His Word, God creates, sustains, re-creates, saves. And the Christian, who finds himself to be a new creation, and knows that what has happened to him is because of the Church's gospel, can say this: what Jesus Christ is, the eternal Word is. In Christ is man's true knowledge of God.

None of this explains just how it could be. But the overwhelming conviction that the crucified-risen one was divine event unparalleled in world history is manifest. Paul put it this way, some fifty years before the Fourth Gospel with its explicit incarnationalism was written:

> For it is the God who said, "Let light shine out of darkness," who has shone in our hearts to give the light of the knowledge of the glory of God in the face of Christ (II Cor. 4:6).

For centuries Judaism had proclaimed a God whose nature it was in and through history to make Himself known and to accomplish His saving purposes. Supremely and decisively had He done so in one particular event of history, Jesus the Christ!

VI

Who was conceived by the Holy Ghost,
Born of the Virgin Mary

From very early times Christians told of Jesus' wondrous birth. He was God's Savior. How fitting that there should have been signs and portents and special circumstances accompanying his entry into the world. His entire life had been something that God had done; so, too, with his conception and birth:

> The Holy Spirit will come upon you,
> and the power of the Most High will overshadow you;

> therefore the child to be born will be called holy,
> the Son of God (Luke 1:35).

> Now the birth of Jesus Christ took place in this way. When
> his mother Mary had been betrothed to Joseph, before they
> came together she was found to be with child of the Holy
> Spirit (Matt. 1:18).

So, in a manner especially striking and effective, the early
Church underlined Jesus' true humanity and true divinity.

Matthew and Luke both record exact circumstances. The
former tells the story from the standpoint of Joseph, the
latter from Mary's perspective. Each tells of happenings that
the other does not mention. Apparently we have here different
cycles of tradition. Both Evangelists, however, have the same
concern — the good news that God has visited and redeemed
His people (Luke 1:68).

Why did these stories so soon become a part of the Apostolic
Witness? This is the first question to ask, because it invites
one to look at the narratives as a whole. In this way we shall
have a proper framework for examination of the component
parts. Lifted out of context, the details often seem but fanciful
incidentals which have no importance. Or, conversely, some
elements may be stressed unduly, with the result that there is
a misrepresentation of the total New Testament witness. But
properly viewed, everything about these stories proves to be
an integral and deeply meaningful part of the Christian faith.
Why, then, were these traditions preserved? What do they
affirm?

The first answer, perhaps, comes as something of a surprise:
Jesus was truly human. Who, we say, would doubt it? Yet
people did, even Christians. It was not the fact that there was
a Jesus of Galilee that was questioned, but something much

more subtle — denial that he was a real person like ourselves.

At first, no one dreamed otherwise. Since there was no need to stress the obvious, our earliest New Testament books say little about it one way or another. We find, to be sure, such phrases as "descended from David according to the flesh," God sent His Son "in the likeness of sinful flesh," or "being born in the likeness of men" (Rom. 1:3; 8:3; Phil. 2:7). But these are not statements consciously theological. It was later, when there were many Gentiles in the Church still unreconciled to the Jewish-Christian insistence upon the fundamental goodness and importance of the phenomenal world as a medium of divine revelation and accomplishment, that the problem arose.[1] And in the Fourth Gospel, the Evangelist's statement, "the Word became flesh" is specifically aimed against an incipient Docetism (from the Greek verb *dokein,* "to seem") which claimed that Jesus of Nazareth only seemed to be a genuine human person (John 1:14).[2] In I John there is a particularly strong indictment of this view: "every spirit which does not confess Jesus [to have come in the flesh] is not of God. This is the spirit of antichrist. . . ." (4:2, 3; cf. II John 7).

Docetism was something aimed at the very heart of the Christian faith, and for that matter was one of the circumstances which forced the Church in post-New Testament times to clarify and formulate her Christology more precisely. That Jesus was truly man is, to put it one way, just what Christianity is all about — God, that is, meets us here where we are, in *this* world. It does not appear that the infancy traditions were in the earliest days told and retold as conscious anti-Docetic

[1] See above, pp. 32–4.
[2] Docetism took many forms, and had its origin in that dualism, prevalent in the Mediterranean world of the day, which looked upon matter as evil. Thus, the divine Son of God must have been pure spirit, at no time really identified with fleshly humanity. One common view, for example, held that the divine Christ descended upon the human Jesus at his baptism, and then departed before his death on the cross. Many of the documents in the New Testament Apocrypha have a Docetic Christology. It was for this reason, among others, that they were not admitted into the canonical New Testament.

polemic. But as the years passed, this was one of the vital purposes which they served, and appropriately so. For they do underline Jesus' humanity with a highly effective artistry.

It is particularly in the small details, the touches of realism, that we see this. Jesus, for example, was born when Herod was King of Judea, and specifically in Bethlehem because of Caesar's decree that adults in Palestine should return to their place of birth for the taking of a census (Luke 1:5; 2:1–5). Joseph, at least ostensibly his father, was an artisan, perhaps a carpenter (Matt. 13:55). The infant was wrapped in "swaddling cloths" and laid "in a manger, because there was no place for them in the inn" (Luke 2:7). The child had known relatives in Elizabeth, her husband Zechariah, and their son John the Baptist, for Elizabeth was Mary's kinswoman (Luke 1:36). Like every male Jew he was circumcised on the eighth day and given a name (Luke 2:21). His mother submitted to the ritual purification customary after childbirth (Luke 2:22–24).

It is only too easy to sentimentalize over such intimate details — which is precisely our point. All of it was and is so real that people can identify themselves with it — which, again, is what the Incarnation is all about. Jesus was truly man.

But Jesus was also Messiah and divine Son sent from God. The entire New Testament witnesses to this fact. The infancy narratives do so with dramatic effectiveness.

The messiahship, for example, is stressed in Matthew's tradition by frequent reference to Old Testament prophecy. The Gospel cites the Septuagint version of Isaiah 7:14:

> Behold, a virgin shall conceive and bear a son, and his name shall be called Emmanuel . . .

These words are applied directly to Mary's child:

> All this took place to fulfill what the Lord had spoken by
> the prophet.

It is, in other words, Jesus whose name is "God with us" (Matt. 1:22, 23). At long last God has fulfilled His promise; Messiah has come.

Matthew also cites Micah 5:2:

> And thou Bethlehem, in the land of Judah, art by no
> means least among the rulers of Judah; for from thee shall
> come a ruler who will govern my people Israel (2:6).

And in Bethlehem, tradition says, Jesus was born, further substantiation of his messiahship.

Hosea 11:1 is also cited: "Out of Egypt have I called my son" (Matt. 2:15). The prophetic reference is to the Exodus under Moses which delivered the forebears of Judaism from bondage in Egypt. Often in New Testament times the newness of Christian lives was spoken of in terms of deliverance from enslavement to the old ways, something accomplished by Jesus the Messiah. So Matthew's tradition understands Hosea's reference as "Messianic prophecy," and sees the story of the holy family's return to Palestine after their flight to Egypt, the land of the Exodus, as yet another indication that Jesus is the Christ.

In Matthew (and Luke as well) we have genealogies which trace Jesus' line of physical descent from the seed of David — another "proof" that he is God's expected anointed one (Matt. 1:1–16; Luke 3:23–38). The Apostle Paul, too, knows of such a tradition. Jesus is God's Son "who was descended from David according to the flesh" (Rom. 1:3). And many years later the anonymous author of II Timothy writes, "Remember Jesus Christ, risen from the dead, descended from David . . ." (2:8).

But the Lucan tradition, too, proclaims that Jesus is God's fulfillment of Israel's hope. In this Gospel, for example, details with respect to his conception and birth are interspersed with parallel accounts of John the Baptist's entry into the world. Why this interest in John? His vocation, we are told, was "to make ready for the Lord a people prepared" — prepared for God's Messiah (Luke 1:17). And Jesus is the Messiah. All four Gospels speak at considerable length about the Baptist — and with this one point in mind. John's task is to herald "the Christ." And even before his birth, he "leaped in [Elizabeth's] womb" for joy when the mother of Jesus visited with her kinswoman (Luke 1:41).

From the angel Gabriel, Mary learns that the child to be born will be given "the throne of his [fore]father David . . . and of his kingdom there will be no end" (Luke 1:32 f.). Jesus is the second David long awaited by Israel. Mary's song (the "Magnificat") pictures the idyllic conditions expected to prevail when the final age of history dawns — and it is her son who will fulfill this divine promise (Luke 1:46–55).[3] It is, the shepherds in the fields are told, the Messiah who has just been born in Bethlehem, the city of David (Luke 2:11); and the ancient Simeon, who had been promised he would not die before he had laid eyes upon the Lord's Messiah, acclaimed the infant Jesus as the answer to his hopes: "Lord, now [at last, for mine eyes have seen him] lettest thou thy servant depart in peace according to thy word" (Luke 2:26–32).[4]

To know Jesus as the Christ is to know God's salvation. This is the witness of the birth stories in both Gospels, a witness identical with that of all the rest of the New Testament. Specially stressed, of course, is the fact that Jesus' *entire* earthly existence has this significance. The manger, no less than the cross, is the visible expression of the God whom Jesus proclaimed as graciously concerned for His world. "Who for us men and for our salvation came down from heaven, And was incarnate of the Holy Ghost of the Virgin Mary, And was

[3] B.C.P., p. 26.
[4] The "Nunc dimittis," B.C.P., p. 28.

made man" — this is the way the Nicene Creed refers to it. It is no wonder that many Christians, when they recite these words, bow the knee. More vividly than anywhere else in the New Testament the infancy narratives reveal the richness of Jewish Messianism and the intensity of feeling which lay behind it, and behind the Christian confession as well.

But there is another significant feature of these traditions — repeated reference to the Holy Spirit.

It was the Spirit that occasioned the conception of Jesus: "The Holy Spirit will come upon you, and the power of the Most High [synonymous with the Spirit] will overshadow you" (Luke 1:35). In the same vein, Matthew's Gospel states that "before they came together she was found to be with child of the Holy Spirit" (1:18). And Joseph's doubts are dispelled by the angel's announcement to him in a dream that "that which is conceived in her is of the Holy Spirit" (1:20). Luke, moreover, says that it was the Spirit which enabled Simeon to recognize the infant Jesus as the Messiah when Mary brought him to the temple (2:26 f.). The same tradition hymns John the Baptist as one whose life "even from his mother's womb" is guided by that Spirit (1:15, 17, 80). He too, as forerunner, is a part of God's plan of salvation.

Judaism had for centuries anticipated the coming of the Kingdom as a time when God's powerful activity (the Spirit) would become strikingly and dramatically apparent. Messiah, too, would be one specially endowed with "power from on high." Both Jesus and his followers had seen the earthly ministry as manifest evidence of that divine power sweeping into people's lives. It was that same Spirit, the first Christians believed, which dominated their lives after the Resurrection.[5]

Again then, the testimony of the birth narratives is that

[5] The role of the Spirit is discussed in detail in connection with the third Article, and particularly pp. 160–64, 169–74, 180–90.

of the total Apostolic Witness. Here is the same good news which is the very *raison d'être* of the entire New Testament — with Jesus of Nazareth there began at last the long-awaited time of salvation. Not simply now and then, not just in this or that or even several particular words and actions, but beginning with conception itself he had been "of the Holy Spirit," and so the long-desired one whose coming would signify the advent of "the last days." To know him, wherever and whenever, was to know in most immediate sense the demand and the blessing of God's reign as King.

The Apostolic Witness also proclaimed the Messiah as the Son of God. Very early, as we have seen, believers were impelled to understand this in terms of a unique divine sonship. To this, too, the infancy narratives bear witness. Quite literally, Jesus was born of a virgin; the role played by the Spirit precluded the operation of a human father. This is the New Testament's most graphic proclamation of Jesus' divinity.

Luke and Matthew are the only sources of information. Mark makes no mention of a supernatural conception. Neither does John, whose opening words hymn Jesus as the incarnation of the pre-existent divine Logos and make no comment as to precisely how "the Word became flesh." These two Evangelists doubtless knew stories which told of unusual circumstances with respect to Jesus' human origin, but did not consider them germane to the immediate purposes for which they took pen in hand. There is no mention of a miraculous conception in the remainder of the New Testament.[6]

[6] In Gal. 4:4 Paul says that "God sent forth his Son, born of a woman, born under the law . . ." — a perfectly natural way of referring to anyone's birth. One does wonder if this text (and others sometimes cited which seem even less promising) would suggest a virgin birth to anyone who did not already know of such a phenomenon by benefit of other sources.

In Mark 6:3 we read, "Is not this the carpenter, the son of Mary and brother

Luke and Matthew compiled their Gospels during the last two decades of the first century. This does not mean, however, that there was no knowledge of a virginal birth until that time. Surely the stories which these two Evangelists relate (and there must have been others now lost to us) circulated by word of mouth for many years before attaining written form. On the other hand, we do have hints that in some circles, and for a considerable period of time, the story of a miraculous conception was unknown.[7] And it is evident that Christians did not, in the earliest days, emphasize the virgin birth as something to be believed "for salvation."

This last is apparent from the fact that we have no reference to a supernatural birth in the places, where, especially, one might expect it — in the samples of early Christian preaching, catechesis, liturgy and hymnology which are embedded in the New Testament text. In preaching and catechesis, especially that designed for potential converts, one generally instructs hearers in fundamentals. In liturgy and hymns it is usually a community's consensus with respect to the things nearest and dearest in matters of faith and piety which is expressed. And yet, in such materials there is no hint.

That Jesus had been born of a virgin may well have been part of the common parlance of popular Christianity from

of James and Joses and Judas and Simon, and are not his sisters here with us?" This may be a pointed reference to the virgin birth. Matthew, however, says at this point (and this gospel *does* have the story of miraculous conception!), "Is not this the carpenter's son? Is not his mother called Mary?" (13:55). Moreover, some early manuscripts of Mark's Gospel at 6:3 refer to Jesus (as does Matthew!) as the son of the carpenter (cf. John 6:42). Whatever the reasons, that there was confusion on this matter is self-evident.

[7] One example is the possible pre-history of the variant readings to Mark 6:3 noted in the preceding footnote. There is also the puzzling fact that Jesus' family seems to have been baffled by his ministry (John 7:5, and Mark 3:21 as rendered by the N.E.B. marginal reading). This seems strange in the light of the virgin birth tradition. Early descriptions of Jesus as "descended from David according to the flesh" (Rom. 1:3; II Tim. 2:8; the genealogies in Matt. 1:1–16 and Luke 3:23–38) are most likely to have originated among Christians who did not know of a virgin birth. Paul's failure to make mention of it is best understood in this way.

very early times. Doubtless such stories played a role in winning others to faith. But it is clear that the earliest preaching of the gospel, the earliest "theology," centered upon the saving death and Resurrection, the mighty words and deeds of Jesus, not upon the "how" of his birth. And it is equally certain that his first followers hailed him as Messiah not because of stories, factual or otherwise, about a supernatural conception, but because of his Resurrection, and the total impact of his remembered and continuing presence with them. The virgin birth was not a crucial issue in the faith and life of the earliest Church.

It is generally recognized today that the historian cannot demonstrate whether or not the biological detail was a literal fact. Such evidence as he has to work with is far from decisive. Moreover, it is not the kind of evidence which can ever answer such a question. We know, too, that there are other considerations quite distinct from those within the competence of the historian which have to be taken into account.

What, for example, does the Church actually mean by "divine sonship"? To answer this requires that one delve into an entirely new area, that of semantics. What, that is, is the nature of language, and particularly of religious language? And what is the relationship between truths and realities, and the thought forms — be they verbal or pictorial — with which we seek to express them? Is there in fact an inevitable equation between Jesus' divine sonship and virgin birth as a literal biological phenomenon, or is, perhaps, the truth to which the tradition would lead us something much deeper?

Then, of course, one's understanding of the doctrine of the Incarnation will inevitably enter into the picture. This, as we know, takes its origin from the *total* Apostolic Witness, and not solely from the infancy narratives, much less from any one specific detail which they contain. And that total witness proclaims and explains the deep meaningfulness of the Jesus of history in a multitude of ways, the one constant being not birth of a virgin, but his uniqueness as God's salvation. For some it seems highly fitting, and so to be expected, that he whom they believe to be divine should be conceived in an unparalleled manner. Others, however, underlining the fact that Jesus' life had as its purpose God's revelation of Himself in terms which we can understand, and thus through the instrumentality of a human person, hold that as truly one of us Jesus must have been conceived and born as are we.

It is awareness of the fact that there is such wide scope in this matter that leads people today to ask further questions, and these two which are especially telling. If, first of all, Jesus was literally born of a virgin, does it really prove more than the fact that in this particular instance parthenogenesis occurred? Clearly, to know that Jesus' manner of birth was unusual does not prove that he was uniquely of God.[8] And the other query is this: Suppose that we should learn beyond all doubt that Joseph was, as a biological fact, his father, how possibly does this disprove the testimony that is written large on every page of the New Testament — that Jesus is the manifest expression of all that God wills and does for man. There are no easy answers to any of these questions. But many today feel that to postulate a *necessary* connection between divine sonship and supernatural conception, and to insist that the truth or falsehood of two thousand years of Christian witness stands or falls on this point, is little short of incredible.

Always the basic questions have been, "Who was this Jesus?

[8] Arguments sometimes put forward on the basis of parthenogenesis as a fact of the natural order are especially dubious. The concern of the proponents is to establish Jesus' uniqueness by adducing further evidence that the biblical story is rooted in fact. But does not parthenogenesis as a natural possibility undercut that which it is hoped to prove? All this suggests something of the futility of arguing pros and cons with respect to the biological detail.

What has God done here?" And the fundamental Apostolic Witness, rooted in the experience of people who were actually there, proclaimed that Jesus Christ was God's salvation. This proclamation took many forms, among which the birth stories in Luke and Matthew were (and are) especially vivid examples. To know Jesus in *every* aspect of his earthly existence is to know God's Savior. It is for this reason that the stories of Mary and Joseph and the Angel Gabriel are still today an integral and compelling part of the Christian gospel. But neither for the first Christians, nor for the Church today, is the fundamental answer to the fundamental question, "born of the *Virgin* Mary."

The claim that Jesus is truly human, truly divine is really a paradox. Over the years the Church has held that both affirmations state something absolutely essential for right and full apprehension of the work and person of Jesus Christ. And this same paradox is present and unresolved in the infancy narratives. Probably the Evangelists were not aware of the problem that it raises, for theological implications of the kind which we have noted had not as yet entered into the thought life of the early Church. But there it stands. Jesus was truly one with us, and yet uniquely of God — and this is the way the Apostolic Witness leaves it.

VII

[Who for us men and for our salvation] Suffered under Pontius Pilate, Was crucified, dead, and buried

"Suffered . . . crucified . . . dead . . . buried" — here is underlined the tragic reality of Jesus' humanity. "Father, if thou art willing, remove this cup from me"; "My God, my God, why has thou forsaken me?"; "he came to his own home, and his own people received him not" (Luke 22:42; Mark 15:34; John 1:11).

Pontius Pilate, before whom Jesus witnessed "the good confession" of a martyr's death, was procurator of Judea from A.D. 26 to 36 (I Tim. 6:13). The mention of his name in a formal Creed seems almost incongruous; but the reminder here that Jesus' birth, life, and death are a matter of record is important. Christianity is rooted in real history.

More than this, however, such a detail underlines that understanding of history which is the common heritage of Judaism and Christianity. The world that God created is the scene of His continuing Lordship. Peoples and events, all phenomena of earthly existence, are media of His purposes. All history is "salvation history." [1] This includes, too, the procuratorship of Pilate. Even here there was a meaning which goes beyond human seeing. Pilate and Herod, Acts declares, did "whatever [God's] hand and [God's] plan had predestined to take place" (4:28). It was "for us men and for our salvation" that Pilate ruled, because, above all else, it was what happened on that last grim weekend which led Jesus' followers to know him as Savior.

Jesus' premature death was all but inevitable. Looking back, we can see this clearly.

Initially, he attracted considerable attention. His mighty works, and especially the prophetic authority with which he acted and spoke set him apart. "We never saw anything like this!" "No man ever spoke like this man!" (Mark 2:12; John 7:46). Many listened and followed. But in all this were present the guarantees of tragedy. For both fame and authority alarmed the religious and civil leaders in Jerusalem.

Frequently, Jesus' incisive words were critical of the formalized Judaism of his day: "Woe to you, scribes and Pharisees,

[1] See above, pp. 32–43 f.

hypocrites!" (Matt. 23:15). His willing and joyous association with those unwilling or unable to adhere to the minutiae of Jewish legalism, over and beyond challenging the laws of ritual purity, seemed a threat to an ordered society: "Why does he eat and drink with tax collectors and sinners?" (Mark 2:16). With respect to the Sabbath and to marriage he not only criticized the tradition, but even presumed to reinterpret the sacred Scriptures upon which that tradition was based (Mark 2:23–28; 10:2–12). He proclaimed God's imminent judgment upon Israel. To be sure, the stern note was more than balanced by stress upon mercy and love, but a love so radical in its implications and demands that even it pointed an accusing finger at the *status quo*. From the beginning, there had been sharp controversy and tension.

There was the political factor also. The ultra-conservative Sadducees were on the whole quite ready to co-operate with the Roman overlords. The Pharisees were far less complacent, but preferred patient endurance to acts of overt rebellion, hoping against hope that God would act soon. And both groups, noting the stir which surrounded Jesus' mission, were apprehensive lest the imperial officials become alarmed. To the latter, as we have seen, rumors of a "King-Messiah" sounded like subversion.

Jesus' following, then, dwindled. For the more apparent became the disfavor of those in authority, the less enthusiastic the "hangers-on." Besides, did he not consistently refuse to assume the role of Messiah? [2] But the rumors kept circulating — and the suspicions. And Jesus knew that if he persisted in his mission, there would be consequences.

He did persist, and before many weeks had passed he began to tell those few who remained that he "must suffer many things, and be rejected by the elders and the chief priests and the scribes, and be killed" (Mark 8:31). "Are you able to drink the cup that I drink, or to be baptized with the baptism with

[2] See above, pp. 46–50.

which I am baptized?" (Mark 10:38). "If any man would come after me, let him deny himself and take up his cross and follow me" (Mark 8:34).

Figuratively and literally, he turned his face towards the focal point of Judaism: "Nevertheless I must go on my way today and tomorrow and the day following; for it cannot be that a prophet should perish away from Jerusalem" (Luke 13:33). At the time of the Passover soon to come the city would be thronged. Here he would speak forth more boldly than ever. Perhaps — there was just a chance — it was this for which God was waiting. The Kingdom would still come. But he was prepared for the worst. If complete obedience to God's will demanded it, if only in this way could God's purposes be accomplished, he would die.

The entry into Jerusalem on the day which we call "Palm Sunday" rekindled the hopes of some. "Hosanna! blessed be he who comes in the name of the Lord!" (Mark 11:9). So he was greeted — as a king about to assert his power and reign. But apparently at the time no one took particular notice of the beast upon which he rode — an ass.

It may have been chance. But in all probability, like the prophets of earlier times Jesus was dramatizing his gospel:[3]

> Rejoice greatly, O daughter of Zion!
> Shout aloud, O daughter of Jerusalem!
> Lo, your king comes to you;
> triumphant and victorious is he,
> humble and riding on an ass,
> on a colt the foal of an ass (Zech. 9:9).

Matthew's account cites this passage, one which may well have

[3] Often the prophets acted out their messages. So, for example, Jeremiah wore a yoke around his neck as proclamation of the necessity of submitting to Nebuchadnezzar, the king of Babylonia (Jer. 27:2–12; cf. I Sam. 15:27,28, I Kings 11:30–32, II Kings 13:15–19, Is. 20:2–4, Ez. 37:15–23). Prophetic symbolism helps us to understand the actions of Jesus in connection with such incidents as the miraculous feeding of the multitudes, and the Last Supper.

been in Jesus' mind as he entered the city (21:1–11). It is God who reigns; and the crisis that Jesus proclaimed was that his people must let Him do so. If he himself, Jesus, were in any sense a king, it was because he confronted his hearers with this authoritative word, and more, in every aspect of his lowly servant life — his forgiveness, his concern for others, his love, his complete obedience to God — was the "incarnation" and the way ("follow me!") of that life in which God does reign, no matter what the cost. And Jesus rode to his death.

For the stir caused by his entry into the city alarmed the authorities even further. Crowds are easily excitable. The entire city could be inflamed. And Jesus' audacity in driving the traders out of the temple precincts and the stern challenge of his teaching, more authoritative and critical and radical than ever before during these last days, sealed the verdict. This could not go on.

The betrayal of Judas, the denial of Peter, the desertion of the other disciples, the indifference and the agony — the tragedy of these events is doubly poignant against the backdrop of Jesus' unshakable faith and uncompromising refusal to forsake what he knew to be God's equally uncompromising will and demand for His world. And so between two thieves he was crucified as a common criminal.

By all rights this should have ended the matter. It might be, his condemners doubtless realized, that Jesus' death as a martyr would occasion a few outcries. But his followers were few in number and had been little in evidence during the last hours. The whole thing would blow over with a minimum of embarrassment. And when such proved not to be the case, still there was no reason to alter the judgment that Jesus had been a well-intentioned but troublesome visionary. The very fact that even after Good Friday his followers continued to take him so seriously only proved their point. It was good that they had stopped it when they had. And, of course, what was being said — "this Jesus did God raise up" — was scandalous. Everybody knew what the Scripture said: "Cursed be every one who hangs on a tree" (Gal. 3:13; cf. Dt. 21:23). To declare that Jesus was God's Messiah was patently absurd.

Saul of Tarsus thought it absurd, too. Whether or not he had ever laid eyes upon Jesus during the earthly ministry we cannot be certain. But he tells us himself that he had been "extremely zealous" for the traditions of his Jewish forebears, and vigorously persecuted this Christian absurdity: "For you have heard of my former life in Judaism, how I persecuted the Church of God violently and tried to destroy it" (Gal. 1:13,14,23; cf. I Cor. 15:9).

But Paul had been set apart for a different task. On the road to Damascus, whither he was journeying with a commission to arrest members of the new sect, he himself saw the risen Lord — and understood that the tree of Calvary was no less than the power and wisdom of God, the very essence of God's purpose and way for His world (I Cor. 1:23–25).

VIII

The third day he rose again from the dead

Some twenty years after his conversion, Paul wrote to the Christians at Corinth:

> Now if Christ . . . has not been raised, then our preaching
> is in vain and . . . your faith is futile and . . . we are of
> all men most to be pitied (I Cor. 15:12–19).

Nothing could be clearer. The Resurrection of Jesus is an indispensable foundation stone of Christianity.[1] It was this that

---

[1] The phrase "He descended into hell" will be discussed at a later point. See pp. 137–41 f.

removed all doubts about the past; and it was this — their present vivid awareness that Jesus was more than ever now in their midst — that made their hopes for the future so sure. The Kingdom had dawned, and the end of all things was gloriously at hand.

According to the Gospel tradition, Jesus himself foretold in detail the events of the Good Friday weekend: "And he began to teach them that the Son of man must suffer many things, and be rejected by the elders and the chief priests and the scribes, and be killed, and after three days rise again" (Mark 8:31; cf. 9:31, 10:33,34). He, of course, realized that tragedy was imminent. But such precise foretelling as this comes from the tradition of the later Church when Christians knew the whole story, and assumed that his divinity meant this kind of omniscience. For still clearly apparent in the Gospels is evidence that the Resurrection took Jesus' closest followers by complete surprise.

Thomas was not the only doubter (John 20:24–29). Luke records that when the women told the apostles about discovering the empty tomb, "these words seemed to them an idle tale, and they did not believe them" (24:10,11). On the road to Emmaus two followers were chided by the risen Jesus (whom they did not recognize!): "O foolish men, and slow of heart to believe all that the prophets have spoken" (Luke 24:25)! Moreover, there is every indication that immediately after the Crucifixion (probably before, in the case of some) the disciples hastened back to Galilee where most of them lived.[2] They expected nothing. It was all over and done with.

What actually happened? How did the earliest believers understand and explain it? Inevitably one thinks first of the empty tomb and appearances as described in the four gospels. These circumstantial narratives, however, are but a part — and

[2] According to Matthew and the spurious ending of Mark (16:9–20), the appearances of Jesus occurred in Galilee. Luke locates such manifestations in and around Jerusalem. The Fourth Gospel combines the two traditions. The "Galilean" tradition is probably the older.

not the most important part, at that — of the total Apostolic Witness.

These words are of special importance:

> For I delivered to you as of first importance what I also received, *that Christ died for our sins in accordance with the scriptures, that he was buried, that he was raised on the third day in accordance with the scriptures, and that he appeared to Cephas, then to the twelve.* Then he appeared to more than five hundred brethren at one time, most of whom are still alive, though some have fallen asleep. Then he appeared to James, then to all the apostles. Last of all, as to one untimely born, he appeared also to me (I Cor. 15:3-8, italics mine.)

Here is our earliest written evidence as to what happened. Moreover, the italicized portion (verses 3b–5) has particular significance, because here we have not Paul's own words, but his quotation of a formula, some kind of primitive minimal summary of a "credal" or catechetical or liturgical nature.[3] In other words, such details as this portion contains were considered to have special importance for faith and proclamation.

In this all too brief formula we have but one notation which suggests how the disciples came to the realization that God had raised Jesus — the phrase "he appeared." As far as proof was possible, here was the point of stress. This apparently is

---

[3] I Cor. was written *c.* A.D. 52–54. But vss. 3b–5, as citation material, must have originated at a considerably earlier date. Set formulae do not grow up overnight. This is, then, by all odds the earliest extant account which we possess that contains any details. Behind the resurrection narratives which the Evangelists record there lies a long oral tradition. But it is much more difficult to speak with any precision about materials in a pre-literary stage. Paul's penned words, then, and particularly the set formula of vss. 3b-5, are of special interest. See p. 93 f. for an earlier brief notation as to the importance of such citation materials.

what Paul considered most important, too. For his own addition to the formula (verses 6–8) underlines the same fact that people, still for the most part alive, had seen the risen Jesus.

Of special interest in this connection is the particular Greek verb which is used, ōphthē (he appeared, was seen). This is a technical word employed by the Septuagint to describe theophanies or divine revelation of a reality which is quite other than that of our own concrete existence.[4] That which, because it is "spiritual," cannot be seen with the naked eye, nevertheless can be discerned, known. Moreover, what is revealed is as "objectively" real and reliable as is anything that can be observed by physical sight.

As used by Paul and the formula, then, the phrase "he appeared" suggests much more than what first occurs when we read it. The appearances of the risen Christ were "theophanies." He who was seen was the one who had been exalted and glorified by God after his death.[5] Now reigning in heaven, he graciously deigned to manifest himself — and in many different ways, just as in the Hebraic frame of reference divine revelation occurs under numerous guises. Thus, to "see" the risen Jesus could mean many things. And that it did is borne out when we look closely at the Apostolic Witness.

Paul, for example, used the formula word with respect to himself: "Last of all . . . he appeared (ōphthē) also to me" (vs. 8). This, he insists, was an appearance every bit as real as that vouchsafed to those who had companied with Jesus in Galilee and Judea. For that matter, he stakes his apostleship on

---

[4] See, for example, Gen. 12:7; Ex. 20:18; Dt. 4:9; Is. 66:18; Amos 1:1; etc.
[5] In this connection, the frequent use of the Greek word doxa (glory) as a description of the risen Christ is significant. See I Cor. 2:8, II Cor. 3:18, 4:4–6, Phil. 3:21, I Tim. 3:16, Luke 24:26, etc. Although having many derived meanings, in both Old and New Testaments, "glory" is something which, ultimately and properly, is characteristic of God who is wholly other. It is the glory of God which can be apprehended by man (Ex. 24:16 f.; Ps. 97:6; Is. 24:23; Ez. 1:28; etc.). Quite apart from important Christological considerations, to speak of Jesus' "glorification" is to point to his risen existence as one which is discerned by theophany.

it: "Am I not an apostle? have I not seen (*ŏphthē*) Jesus our Lord?" (I Cor. 9:1; cf. 15:9,10). And Paul's "seeing" appears to have been of a visionary character. In Acts the story is told three times: "suddenly a light from heaven flashed about him. And he fell to the ground and heard a voice saying to him, 'Saul, Saul, why do you persecute me?'" (9:3–7; 22:6–11; 26:13–19). In Galatians he himself terms it a "revelation" (1:11–17). This was theophany. The risen one now enjoys that realm of existence which is so different from our own.

Then there is the reference to an appearance "to more than five hundred brethren at one time" (vs. 6). It has been suggested that this points to a "Pentecostal" type of phenomenon of the sort described in Acts: "And when they had prayed, the place in which they were gathered together was shaken; and they were all filled with the Holy Spirit and spoke the word of God with boldness" (4:31; cf. 2:1–13).

This hypothesis, although tentative, is a shrewd one. In the first place, the New Testament contains several early and intriguing texts which associate *dunamis* (power) and/or Spirit with Jesus' Resurrection or risen state.[6] And more generally, and repeatedly (and this as late as the writing of the Fourth Gospel), Christian writers speak in virtually identical and interchangeable terms of the work of the Spirit and the work of the risen Christ. For Paul, to be "in Christ" is to be "in the Spirit."[7] In short, there is the closest possible connection between the Resurrection of Jesus, the Spirit as the mode of his continuing relationship with the world, and the Spirit as the mode of the believer's apprehension of Christ. All this is suggestive.

For one thing, there seems to shine through here the fact that some of Jesus' early followers knew him to have been

[6] See, for example, I Cor. 6:14, II Cor. 13:4, Rom. 1:4, I Tim. 3:16, Acts 1:2, Phil. 3:10. There is, moreover, a close connection between "power" and "glory." In Rom. 6:4, for example, "Christ was raised from the dead by the *glory* of the Father"! See the previous footnote.

[7] See below, pp. 181–7.

raised from the dead because of deeply moving experiences of a charismatic nature. Beyond this, however, one wonders if we may not have here the lingering traces of a more primitive view, one now all but hidden from us — a tradition which knew nothing of an empty tomb, and neither conceived of nor proclaimed Jesus' Resurrection in terms of reconstitution of the same body which hung on the cross. Here again the significance of ōphthē comes to mind. And the evidence will suggest to some the possibility that the Easter event was actually a phenomenon which did not involve displacement of the earthly body.[8] This would mean that the new glorified state which followed upon the Crucifixion was revealed as a theophany, and in manifold ways — a theophany none the less true in what it revealed, and the exaltation of Jesus no less a fact, for all that the new risen life involved a kind of reality beyond our own immediate observation, and for all that it was, therefore, the working of the Spirit rather than a naked eye seeing that impelled the resurrection faith, and the changed lives which confirmed that faith.[9]

The Gospel narratives of the appearances represent a tradition more immediately concerned with the "how" of the theophany. And yet even here Jesus' manifestation of himself is effected in different ways to different people. Beneath this

[8] This, of course, requires further consideration of the empty tomb tradition. See below, pp. 112–14.

[9] Another element of the most primitive tradition, also suggesting the comprehensiveness of the verb ōphthē, is the fact that some of the earliest proclamations of God's mighty act spoke not specifically of "resurrection," but rather of exaltation, glorification, or immediate session at God's right hand. In one case, Phil. 2:8,9, reference to Christ's death is complemented by reference to "exaltation." In others, although "resurrection" is sometimes mentioned in the immediate context, alternate ways of speaking of the transformation are used (for example, I Tim. 3:16; I Pt. 3:18; Acts 2:33; 3:13; 5:31; Heb. 1:3; 5:5–10). Again, the close connection between the Resurrection and "glory" should be noted.

tradition also there lie different kinds of seeing experience.

One group of stories strongly underlines the corporeal reality of Jesus' new life. Such is the concern of these words:

> And he said to them, "Why are you troubled, and why do questionings rise in your hearts? See my hands and my feet, that it is I myself; handle me, and see; for a spirit has not flesh and bones as you see that I have." And while they still disbelieved for joy, and wondered, he said to them, "Have you anything here to eat?" They gave him a piece of broiled fish, and he took it and ate before them (Luke 24:38–43; cf. John 20:27).

The chief concern here is to refute the charge of disbelievers that the risen Christ was merely a wraith of the imagination or, as perhaps some Christians themselves believed, simply a ghost lacking any significant continuity with the earthly figure.[10] On the contrary, he whom they had seen was unmistakably the same Jesus whom they had earlier known, shared physical hardship with, loved.

We turn now to another text:

> When he was at table with them, he took the bread and blessed, and broke it, and gave it to them. And their eyes were opened and they recognized him. . . . (Luke 24:30,31; cf. John 21:13).

This passage points to a different circumstance in which followers attained to the Resurrection faith — the breaking of bread. Often during the earthly ministry Jesus and his disciples had shared meals together. And on the night of his betrayal, by word and gesture he had given to this act such significance that from that time on for one Christian to break bread with another was inescapably to recall him.[11] It is, then,

---

[10] This is to point to an anti-Docetic motif. See above, pp. 86–8.
[11] See below, pp. 166–9.

of particular significance that the two who traveled on the road to Emmaus told others "how he was known to them in the breaking of the bread" (Luke 24:35). Note, too, that both Luke 24:30 and John 21:13 show traces of primitive Eucharistic language.[12] Christians, Peter tells Cornelius, "ate and drank with [Jesus] after he rose from the dead" (Acts 10:41). All this suggests that the repeated eating motif of the Resurrection stories has more behind it than simply the demonstration of continuity between the "before" and the "after." Still farther in the background lies the fact that it was in their breaking of bread together after Good Friday that Jesus manifested himself to his followers. In this way many saw him.

Always it was the same Jesus. Nevertheless, there was a difference, as they well knew. And one wonders how that "otherness" could be expressed in a manner different from that which the tradition employs:

> And their eyes were opened and they recognized him; and he vanished out of their sight (Luke 24:31).

> As they were saying this, Jesus himself stood among them. But they were startled and frightened, and supposed that they saw a spirit (Luke 24:36,37; cf. John 20:19,26).

Here is the precise opposite of the stress upon the corporeality of the risen one. He passes through doors, comes and goes in quite unhuman fashion. He does not himself eat the bread and fish (in contrast to Luke 24:42!) which he distributes to the disciples (Luke. 24:31; John. 21:13).

For all his recognizability, then, the "sameness" had somehow been transformed, become "spiritual." To know him now was to know that which was familiar, and yet totally unfamiliar; it was to encounter a dimension of reality which had been hidden during the earthly ministry.

The fact that these accounts of appearances have contra-

[12] The language, especially that in Luke, should be compared with that of the accounts of the Last Supper and the miraculous feedings.

dictory elements hardly surprises us. They have, to a considerable extent, been shaped by apologetic motifs; each detail has its own purpose, and underlines in its own way that marvel wrought by God which was so fraught with meaning as to defy adequate description. No less than the other materials which we have examined, the Gospel stories describe a theophany. The total Apostolic Witness to the Resurrection is like many different shafts of light all spotted upon one great reality. Jesus' followers saw him in a variety of ways — and all agreed that it was he. There are, as we ourselves well know, many ways in which one sees, discerns, knows. "To them he presented himself alive after his passion by *many* proofs" (Acts 1:3, italics mine). And their lives were set on a new course.

To consider only the Gospel Resurrection narratives is, as we have seen, to ignore much else that is important. Yet another implication of the preceding pages is that merely to argue pros and cons as to what kind of embodiment was involved is sadly to limit our understanding of how the first believers themselves apprehended and proclaimed this mighty action of God. Let us return to Paul for one further hint which many find suggestive.

In I Corinthians 15 we have not only significant early evidence of Jesus' Resurrection, but also the Apostle's detailed description of the resurrection of the individual believer at the last day. This he gives in his famous analogy of the seed in verses 35-38. He makes two points, both important.

The body of this flesh dies and like a seed is sown in the grave, and in God's time there arises a new body. Paul's first concern is clear. That life which is future will be an embodied existence. And between the "before" and the "after" there will be a sameness, an essential continuity.

At the same time, that growth which arises from the implanted seed is new. So, too, will be the Christian's future state.[13] Paul stresses the contrast with such opposites as "perishable-imperishable," "physical-spiritual"; "flesh and blood cannot inherit the kingdom of God."

Can we, from all this, deduce what the Apostle believed as to the nature of Jesus' Resurrection? The following passages are worthy of note:

> But in fact Christ has been raised from the dead, the first fruits of those who have fallen asleep. . . . For as in Adam all die, so also in Christ shall all be made alive. But each in his own order: Christ the first fruits, then at his coming those who belong to Christ (I Cor. 15:20–23; cf. Col. 1:18).

> For if we have been united with him in a death like his, we shall certainly be united with him in a resurrection like his (Rom. 6:5).

> . . . a Savior, the Lord Jesus Christ, who will change our lowly body to be like his glorious body . . . (Phil. 3:20,21).

> For those whom he foreknew he also predestined to be conformed to the image of his Son, in order that he might be the first-born among many brethren (Rom. 8:29).

The first of these passages is the connecting link between the strong reminder of the Church's proclamation of Jesus' Resurrection at the beginning of I Corinthians 15, and the detailing of what happens to the believer in verses 35-57. It is, according to Paul, because God raised Jesus that the person "in Christ"

[13] The seed analogy is not precise. It stands up as far as continuity and "sameness" are concerned. But it is less satisfactory as illustrative of transformation into something *totally* different. But that Paul is also using it to this end is clear from the context: there are different kinds of flesh, different kinds of bodies, different kinds of glories (vss. 38–41). See also vss. 42–50, and especially these words: "It is sown a physical body, it is raised a spiritual body. If there is a physical body, there is also a spiritual body"; "I tell you this, brethren: flesh and blood cannot inherit the kingdom of God, nor does the perishable inherit the imperishable" (vss. 44, 50). For further discussion of this passage, see below, pp. 204–9.

may rest assured of his own resurrection.[14] The other texts stress specifically the similarity between the risen Christian and his Lord.

Now Paul nowhere himself explicitly details the nature of Jesus' risen embodiment. We cannot, therefore, speak with certainty. But it is worthy of note that the Apostle's handling of the seed analogy points to a kind of future state which does not require the displacement of one's earthly remains, and consequently empty graves or tombs. Rather than mechanical equation of "before" and "after," there is transformation of the "before." Beyond the grave, one's own same self is new, and this newness is that of a reality quite other than that which we know at present. And, significantly, this is quite in accord with what we have found from examination of the witness with respect to the risen Jesus — strong underlining of the sameness of the crucified-risen one, and yet every indication that the first Christians understood their discernment of him as a theophany (*ōphthē*), the gracious manifestation of one now of a totally other realm of existence.

Judaism, of course, believed in a concrete embodiment as necessary to meaningful life beyond the grave. And doubtless Paul (and others, too) visualized the exalted Christ as a glorious, but still recognizably human, form in the heavens at God's right hand. How else could one imagine it? But this, of course, only tells us the way people pictured it. The nature of that heavenly existence remains a mystery. And what, precisely, Paul understood with respect to the hidden details of Jesus' Resurrection we can only surmise.

Nevertheless, it is suggestive that he refers obviously and specifically to the "how" of that Resurrection only once (I Cor. 15:1–8) in all his extant writings. Did he perhaps realize that the concrete details of the primitive Church's tradition had only limited value as evidence? Be this as it may, one cannot help feeling that there is significance in the accord between

[14] See below, pp. 202–4.

III

his description of the believer's last day resurrection, and the biblical evidence that the appearances of the risen Jesus were theophanies. Some may be prompted to ask this question: Must one make a precise equation between the truth of the Apostolic Witness — that God raised him from the dead — and the phenomenal details of the Gospel narratives?

And what of the empty tomb? The evidence at first glance seems impressive. All four Evangelists are unanimous that there was such a phenomenon. And although there are contradictions and discrepancies between the various Gospel stories, they are not such as necessarily to impugn the central witness.

A second look, however, gives pause. For one thing, it is significant that the earliest account in I Corinthians says nothing of an empty tomb. Paul makes no mention of it anywhere in his epistles, and apart from the Gospel stories our only New Testament references appear in Acts 2:29 (perhaps) and 13:29. This particular detail certainly did not play a key role in the earliest Resurrection faith or its proclamation.[15]

This is significant quite apart from whether or not the tomb

[15] Again, important is the fact that we do not have references to an empty tomb where we would of all places expect to have them, viz., in the earliest liturgical and catechetical materials (see above, p. 103).

In Acts 2:29, part of Peter's first sermon, the tomb reference, if intended at all, is an implication of mention of David's tomb. In 13:29 there is explicit mention ("they took him down from the tree, and laid him in a tomb"); this is a speech of Paul's at Antioch of Pisidia. The Petrine and Pauline sermons in Acts are, of course, not *ipsissima verba*. They are constructions by the author which incorporate some earlier elements of tradition, but we cannot, with any confidence, claim that the Acts references give us evidence which is earlier than or contemporary with the Resurrection account in I Cor. 15. Nor can I Cor. 15:4 ("he was buried") be taken as our earliest evidence for the empty tomb, as some would do. This *may* be its implication. Knowing about the tomb from other sources, one inevitably thinks of it when reading vs. 4. But we do not know the circumstances under which this formula was constructed, nor what was in the minds of the first users. Many scholars hold that vss. 3b–5 reflect a circle of tradition which, for whatever reason, knew nothing of such a phenomenon.

tradition contains a hard core of truth. Early Christians, one may suspect, were not totally unaware that an empty tomb has little evidential value. What does it prove — other than emptiness? The Gospel stories themselves make this clear. Behind the Matthean tradition, for example, lies just the kind of dialogue which we would expect. As soon as early believers began to talk of the empty tomb, disbelievers, of course, came up with all sorts of suggestions — plausible ones, too — as to the cause. And Christians (also "of course"!) came right back with reasons why their own explanation was the right one.[16]

Again, contradictory details are what one would expect. An intense faith in dialogue with mockers was bound to multiply and magnify those circumstances, whatever they were, which led Jesus' followers to know him as the risen one. But when all is said and done, the empty tomb tradition (or to put it more accurately, the complex of traditions loosely conjoined) has evolved in such a way and to such a degree that the historian cannot say with any certainty what lies behind it.

It is possible, as many have suggested, that this particular phenomenon is best understood as a relatively late addition to the Resurrection tradition. There are any number of ways in which the story could have originated, as well as reasons why it became important as the years went by.[17] This hypothesis provides the most unstrained explanation for the fact that our earliest sources make no reference to the tomb. It also fits with

[16] It was pointed out, for example, that the women could have gone to the wrong tomb. But no, was the Christian reply; there was an angel who bade specifically, "Come, see the place where he lay" (Matt. 28:6). There were others who laughed the matter off by saying that Jesus' body had been stolen. This, too, makes sense — until, that is, one learns that the hostile Jews themselves gained Pilate's consent to place a guard at the entrance of the tomb (Matt. 27:62–66). Someone else, however, said that the guard had fallen asleep. Christians had a ready reply: the guard had been bribed to say this (Matt. 28:11–15)! Moreover, the unusual size of the stone, so great that it could be moved by no human hands, proved that the body could not have been stolen (Matt. 28:2; cf. Mark 16:3 f.). God had miraculously raised him!
[17] To use here the word "fabrication" in its oftentimes derogatory sense would be to misunderstand totally the nature of biblical materials as faith proclamation, as well as to ignore the necessities and manner of religious language.

the other evidence that we have noted — that it may have been the power of the Spirit rather than a literal seeing and touching which impelled the earliest Resurrection faith.[18]

Many, however, with an understandable caution prefer to leave the question open. There is more than one possible reason for the silence of the earliest tradition as to the tomb. Clearly, historical analysis of our present sources does not enable us to say with certainty that it happened this way or that way. And there is nothing in the preceding pages that makes untenable the conclusion that the kind of resurrection depicted in the Gospel narrative is a significant pointer to the nature of this event. Some, then, may wish to go on, and opt for this view: in some manner — for, of course, the mystery remains — God used Jesus' earthly embodiment as a means of revealing that the cross was not the end, but the beginning of a new dimension of existence.

But whatever the answer, the empty tomb tradition has little evidential value for us today. And it is the all but unanimous conviction of scholars that it was the appearances, the fact that Jesus, perhaps in many different ways, was manifested to his own, which demanded the proclamation, "the Lord is risen."

If, as some prefer to think, the Resurrection of Jesus was totally a phenomenon of the spiritual world, then the tradition of reanimation of the same earthly body inevitably accompanied by an empty tomb represents an end result — the "concretization" of a faith which was initially arrived at by spiritual apprehension. And it is possible to suggest something of the "why" and "how" of this process.

Influential, for example, would be the Hebraic understanding of "personhood" as something requiring embodiment. And

[18] See above, pp. 105 f.

most early Christians thought in such terms.[19] To speak of Jesus as still alive was, inevitably, to think of him as having a human form. As a corollary to this, the question, of course, arose, "What does the future hold for us?" And again, how difficult to imagine that future state except in terms of our present. This concern, too, would lead to anthropomorphic descriptions of Jesus' exaltation and new heavenly life.[20]

Another motive behind "concretization" would be the need for a convincing answer to those who laughed off the Christian claims as a mere "ghost story" or wishful thinking. Behind this, however, lay a theological concern which sensed that recognition of the *sameness* of the one who manifested himself after his death was of particular importance. As we have already stressed, the fact that God's revealing and saving action was mediated through the *human* Jesus of Nazareth and Galilee is crucial. It is equally crucial with respect to the Resurrection (both his, and that of the believer)—for resurrection is an integral part of the total divine plan for salvation. Hence the necessity, if indeed that which happened was "for us men and for our salvation," of stressing that the heavenly Christ was the same as he who was crucified, a fact underlined by such tangible things as an empty tomb, being touched, eating, and other similar details.[21]

[19] See above, p. iii, and below pp. 202–7. I Cor. 15, however, appears to have been written as an answer to certain members of the Corinthian Church who were troubled by the concept of the bodily resurrection.
[20] This, incidentally, is especially suggestive for those who are sometimes concerned when led to question a physical resurrection. The initial reaction is to see it as a threat to one's self, simply because it is all but impossible to imagine a future without that present embodiment which, after all, represents the only kind of existence that one knows. Such apprehension, however, is quite unnecessary. What lies ahead is completely other, hence a mystery now. But the crucial point is that *whatever it may be,* one who was flesh and blood like ourselves has gone before. See the next footnote, and below, pp. 207–9 f.
[21] This, again, is the anti-Docetic motif, although strictly speaking one should think in terms of "Docetic tendencies" with respect to the first years of the Church's life. Docetism as a specific Christian heresy appeared later as a phenomenon of growing theological consciousness and formulation. That the

This, perhaps, will suffice by way of illustration. The particular idiom and imagery, of course, reflect an age and a culture very different from our own. Many different factors — historical, theological, apologetic, personal, and, by no means least, that anthropomorphism which is an inevitable corollary of the human circumstance — would have contributed to a need, which must have arisen very early, to explain the Resurrection of Jesus by reference to human corporeality. And perhaps in some such manner as suggested above, his followers came to proclaim, in terms of the only concrete kind of existence that they themselves knew, that which was initially apprehended in the traditional mode of divine revelation. How else, we may ask, could one express it — the unshakable certainty that this theophany was different from all others, that it was the *person* Jesus of Nazareth who was God's salvation?

Behind the New Testament witness to Jesus' Resurrection there lies a complex pre-history. Efforts at reconstruction are all highly tentative. These facts alone suggest caution, and underline the reasonableness of the viewpoint that the Gospel stories offer the best clue as to the character of this event.

At the same time, the caution points in another direction.

divine Christ was fully human, and that it was he *with that full humanity* whom God raised is the *sine qua non*. See above, pp. 86–8.

It should, however, be noted that to postulate the Resurrection of Jesus as a spiritual phenomenon, and his risen state as an utterly other "spiritual" body, is not Docetism! Such a postulation, no less than the more literalistic view, maintains as crucial the fact that it was the *same* Jesus who was transformed into that utterly other existence which no longer employs the fleshly medium of our present experience. Herein lies a significance of Paul's use of the seed analogy (see pp. 109–12 and 204–8). Only a view which denies (against the total biblical and Christian tradition!) that there is such a thing as intangible "objective" reality, that is, only a materialism which equates reality solely with things concrete and phenomenal, will demand that the doctrine of the Incarnation (the eternal Word became flesh) means that that same flesh (whether it be the bodily form of Jesus of Nazareth or our own) remains forever as an essential part of "personhood!"

The stories of tomb and appearances, as we have seen, are but a small part of the biblical witness. Moreover, although they seem to answer some questions, they raise as many others. The fact is that the total Apostolic Witness as to the "how" is inconclusive. One cannot, then, *demand* that people equate the truth of that Witness with empty tomb and physical reanimation of the same body which was taken down from the cross. These circumstantial details need not be the stumbling blocks to faith in the Resurrection which they have become for some.

We may recall here the precise wording of the Apostles' Creed: "the third day he rose again from the dead." This, it should be underlined, is precisely the phrase of the Apostolic Witness. No place do we read "rose from the grave" or "rose from the tomb." The New Testament phrase is *ek tōn nekrōn,* "from among the dead." [22] There is neither demand nor need that any Christian be more specific than this.

The "how" of this mighty action of God, then, remains obscure. And we would suggest here, not that one explanation is necessarily more reasonable or logical than another, but rather that the Resurrection faith may be, and is, appropriated in different ways by different people. No less today, that is, than in former times — and this quite apart from the details — the biblical evidence retains its power to lead the searcher to personal knowledge of the risen Christ. This, too, may be underlined — that the historian poses difficult questions for those who would reject the Apostolic Witness out of hand.

How, for example, is one to account for the gathering together again of the despairing and disillusioned followers of Jesus who had deserted him at the time of his death? What happened to Peter who denied him, that he should turn and become the Church's earliest leader, and finally die for Christ? What occurred to induce the downcast disciples, contrary to all their past experience and expectations as Jews, to proclaim as

[22] See, for example, I Cor. 15:12,20, Col. 1:18, I Th. 1:10, Heb. 13:20; cf. Eph. 5:14.

Savior one who died reviled and cursed on a tree? What happened to make possible for almost two thousand years the weekly, even the daily joyful recalling of a degrading death in the breaking of bread? Suddenly, lives were radically transformed. Where there had been despair, defeatism, there was, almost overnight, excitement and joy and sureness of purpose and hope.

All these are facts which the historian *can* verify. And the Christian finds it inconceivable that behind this there lie only frustrated hopes and wishful thinking. And when all is said and done, the chief witness to the truth of the Resurrection — and it has always been this way — is the existence of the Church and the quality of her life. He who lives the fullness which is the Church's life finds that the Apostolic Witness is true: "God raised Jesus from among the dead"!

IX

"Who was put to death for our trespasses
and raised for our justification" (Rom. 4:25)

Repeatedly the Apostolic Witness declares, "Christ died for us, for our sins." The pages of the New Testament are full of explanations as to how this could be. We today are so far away from the actual historical events, that it is difficult really to comprehend what a startling claim this was. The cross on all counts looked to be the very epitome of frustration and futility, and yet a handful of people, reared in a tradition which said "cursed be every one who hangs on a tree," were claiming that this tree was God's salvation. Here, to say the least, is impressive evidence of the intensity of the Resurrection faith.

One must recall here the lives of the first Christians. Explain it how one will, they were a changed people. Somehow, to know Jesus as God's Messiah had set them on a new path, one as different from the old way as day is from night. At first, they themselves did not know how to explain it, apart from the certainty that it was "because of him." Soon, however, they were talking about this newness as a "dying and rising" with Christ, and specifically of the fact that because of the cross their past had been forgiven.

The Nicene Creed has the phrase "crucified also *for us* under Pontius Pilate." The Apostles' Creed lacks any such personal reference, but the implication is obvious.[1] The world had mocked, but it had all been of God: he was "delivered up for our trespasses, and was raised up for our justification" (Rom. 4:25; A.S.V.). In order to understand this particular idiom, it will be helpful to look again at Jesus' ministry.

In first-century Palestine it was a commonplace to postulate a connection between sin and the tribulations of an individual's life.[2] Not only unfortunate circumstances in general, but quite specifically mental and physical illness were regarded as a direct result of transgressions, punishment for the breaking of divine commands.

Jesus did not believe God to be this kind of angry avenger. He did, however, recognize an intimate association between sin and every facet of human well-being. This view is illustrated by Mark's story of the paralytic. There are two pronouncements: "My son, your sins are forgiven," and "Rise, take up your pallet and walk" (2:1-12). At the root of the man's paralysis was sin. And as we have seen, Jesus understood the mighty works done through him as God's sovereign power now at last breaking Satan's strangle hold upon the peoples of the world.[3]

---

[1] It is partially for this reason that we have interpolated into our format of the shorter formulary the words from the Nicene Creed "who for us men and for our salvation." See above, pp. 30, 32. Note, too, in the Apostles' Creed the phrase in the third Article, "The Forgiveness of sins"; see below, pp. 169–79. (Italics mine.)

[2] This startles us less today than hitherto. Modern psychiatry has added new and valuable insights to the Church's age-old teaching with respect to sin and the right orientation of the lives of individuals.

[3] See above, pp. 54–6.

The literalness of this imagery need not concern us. The fundamental point and its connection with Jesus' central message are apparent. God must and will be King. Man's sin is his refusal, for whatever reason, to accept this fact. Repent; let God reign! To do this, by abnegating the wrong kind of self, is true life of untold meaningfulness.

But over and beyond Jesus' words there was his own life, observably devoid of self and observably lived for others. Even more, there were results. In all kinds of ways people's lives were upturned by knowing him. God's will as King, Jesus proclaimed, is for salvation — wholeness here and now of body and mind. And those who, however dimly, recognized that their sufficiency was not of themselves, and that they had need for what God willed to give, knew salvation not as a theory but as a power actually operative within them.[4] Because of Jesus, new life had in fact come. Their past, their sins had been forgiven.

The first nucleus of Christians included some of those same people who had known him as a "power unto salvation" before Good Friday. And after, they still knew him as Savior, and so, in increasing numbers, did others. Why was it, how could it be that their lives had changed so? He died, they said, as he had lived, for us, for others, his own total denial of self, in order to be the Servant of others, somehow proving to be a power which gives, forgives, re-creates. God's power, this was; and to know God's Servant was to die to the past, and to be apprehended by that love in a new, saved, risen life.

The New Testament has many references to this Death-Resurrection pattern. It was the shape of Jesus' entire life and,

---

[4] Recognition of need, we suggest, is what lies behind the frequent indications in the tradition that some kind of faith was necessary before Jesus could heal. See, for example, Mark 2:5; 5:28; 6:5,6; Luke 7:9; Matt. 9:27–29, etc. It was not ultimately faith in him, but in his gospel which was required — and this not as a kind of formal acceptance or confession, but rather the willingness to admit that to "go it alone" no longer made sense, the desire, however incoherent, to let God take over and reign.

as soon became clear, God's way for Everyman: death to self means a true self. We cite here just one text:

> Do you not know that all of us who have been baptized into Christ Jesus were baptized into his death? We were buried therefore with him by baptism into death, so that as Christ was raised from the dead by the glory of the Father, we too might walk in newness of life (Rom. 6:3 f:).

Jesus' followers never tired of talking about what had happened. And then, over and beyond this, there was the need to explain it so that others might be won. Thus our New Testament proclaims the meaning of the cross in innumerable ways. Let us sample a few.

In Isaiah we read this deeply moving passage:

> Surely he has borne our griefs
>   and carried our sorrows;
> yet we esteemed him stricken,
>   smitten by God, and afflicted.
> But he was wounded for our transgressions,
>   he was bruised for our iniquities;
> upon him was the chastisement that made us whole,
>   and with his stripes we are healed.
> All we like sheep have gone astray;
>   we have turned every one to his own way;
> and the Lord has laid on him
>   the iniquity of us all (53:4–6).

These words the first Christians saw as a picture of Jesus himself, a prophecy of his death for the sins of men.

Who was the sufferer of whom Isaiah wrote? We do not know, nor even if the writer had in mind any particular person. But this tragic figure is set forth in the later chapters of

Isaiah as a symbol of the nation Israel in one of her moments of deepest humiliation.[5] The "Suffering Servant," as he is called, stands as Judaism's deepest penetration into man's perennial problem of tragedy and evil — the awareness that the suffering of one person or group can redeem, can work good for others.

Israel as a nation had been shattered, the flower of her people in exile, the future bleak — and this as a result of her failure to keep covenant with God.[6] But, says the prophet, there is still hope, and in all this tragedy, a divine purpose. If the nation will repent, and hold fast her faith, out of this "death" she will rise again purified, strengthened. But more than this, her steadfastness in present tribulation will be a witness to all the world: "I will give you as a light to the nations, that my salvation may reach to the end of the earth" (Is. 49:6). Israel's death and resurrection will be her redemption, and that of all other peoples, too. For the nations will see that the power of the one God is not an arbitrary despotism, but a love which forgives and re-creates, and that to admit His sovereignty is a prize to be desired beyond anything else.

Did Jesus specifically identify his mission with Isaiah's redemptive Servant? No certain answer is possible. The important thing is that his life did, in fact, correspond to this picture: "the Son of man has nowhere to lay his head"; "I am among you as one who serves" (Luke 9:58; 22:27). And as we have noted so often, his life of concern for others was in fact redemptive. When, as happened almost immediately, Christians pointed to the Servant poems as "prophecies" of Jesus, they were profoundly right.[7] For as sheer fact, knowing him had re-created their lives.

[5] The specific passages embedded in the text and designated as the "Servant Songs" are as follows: 42:1–9; 49:1–13; 50:4–11; 52:13 — 53:12.
[6] See above, pp. 36–8.
[7] The Servant passages were perhaps also taken as prophecy of Jesus' Resurrection. See, for example, Is. 52:13, and such texts as Phil. 2:9 and Rom. 4:25. Acts 2:33, 5:31, John 3:14, 8:28, 12:32 f. also employ the exaltation theme.

This Servant Christology was in all probability the first theology of the cross. The New Testament contains many samples. These are especially familiar:

> He himself bore our sins in his body on the tree, that we might die to sin and live to righteousness. By his wounds you have been healed. For you were straying like sheep, but have now returned to the Shepherd and Guardian of your souls (I Pt. 2:24,25).

> I have been crucified with Christ; it is no longer I who live, but Christ who lives in me; and the life I now live in the flesh I live by faith in the Son of God, who loved me and gave himself for me (Gal. 2:20).

> For you know the grace of our Lord Jesus Christ, that though he was rich, yet for your sake he became poor, so that by his poverty you might become rich (II Cor. 8:9).

> For the Son of man also came not to be served but to serve, and to give his life as a ransom for many (Mark 10:45).

The cross, which of course means Christ's entire life of death to self for others, is God's way unto salvation. It was Jesus' own self-abnegation which had been witnessed and which had re-created the witnesses. To know him as Servant of others was to know that self-sacrificing love is the power of God Himself, and the seemingly futile cross as mediating that power (I Cor. 1:18–25). The cross is essential for salvation, makes possible that which no man can do for himself. For it is precisely at the moment when one dies to self that God's new beginning with forgiveness for the past breaks in.

There were many ramifications of this Servant Christology. The very wonder of the new life compelled believers to explain it in many ways. In the following passages, for example, Christian redemption is thought of in terms of a transaction which makes payment:

> You are not your own; you were bought with a price (I Cor. 6:19,20: cf. 7:23).

> You know that you were ransomed from the futile ways inherited from your fathers, not with perishable things such as silver or gold, but with the precious blood of Christ, like that of a lamb without blemish or spot (I Pt. 1:18,19).

> For there is one God, and there is one mediator between God and men, the man Christ Jesus, who gave himself as a ransom for all . . . (I Tim. 2:5,6).

Behind such texts lies the concept of sin as a power that enslaves. Satan and his agents hold one in thrall, with the result that one is all but powerless to fight back. But Christ has broken this strangle hold. Without himself sinning, he suffered all that the demon powers could do to him, even unto death — and yet rose victorious. So he has forged a way which the man of faith can follow. The slaves have been manumitted; the kidnapped have been ransomed. "You were bought with a price" — the cross.

Beneath the seeming crudeness of some of this imagery are facts not lightly to be brushed aside. God's will is for righteousness. And yet so often one feels helpless and hopeless. But somehow, to know the Christ is to know at one and the same time the certainty of forgiveness and an impelling desire with power to fulfill God's demand. It is not that sin is no more, but the sting of hopeless despair is gone.

Closely related to such "ransom" cross theology is another idiom, one which draws heavily upon the sacrificial practice of the Jewish cultus.[8] Here are some familiar samples:

> In him we have redemption through his blood, the forgiveness of our trespasses, according to the riches of his grace . . . (Eph. 1:7).

> Since, therefore, we are now justified by his blood, much more shall we be saved by him from the wrath of God (Rom. 5:9).

> Cleanse out the old leaven that you may be fresh dough, as you really are unleavened. For Christ, our paschal lamb, has been sacrificed . . . (I Cor. 5:7).

> Behold, the Lamb of God, who takes away the sin of the world (John 1:29)!

> For if sprinkling defiled persons with the blood of goats and bulls and with the ashes of a heifer sanctifies for the purification of the flesh, how much more shall the blood of Christ, who through the eternal Spirit offered himself without blemish to God, purify your conscience from dead works to serve the living God (Heb. 9:13,14).

In these and many other such passages Jesus' death is represented as a sacrifice necessary for the world's reconciliation to God.

Animal sacrifice had long been practised by Judaism in the temple cultus. Its pre-history is complex; but the central concern was the establishment or re-establishment of a right relationship between God and His people. The life of an animal victim (which it was believed resided in the blood) sacrificed to God constituted the self-offering of His people. In this manner covenants were sealed, or the nation repentant for sin

---

[8] All these categories — Servant, ransom, sacrifice, etc. — overlap to a considerable extent.

reconsecrated herself. In earlier times the intent doubtless was to appease an angry deity. Later, however, and this is the New Testament point of view, sacrifice effected expiation ("wiping out") of the sins of the people and so the restoration of peace with God.

So the first Christians knew themselves to be reconciled with God because of their relationship with Christ. His offering of himself had been for them, his blood had wiped out their past, his death had been their reconsecration and made possible their new forgiven lives. Moreover — and this was the amazing thing — it was God Himself who had supplied the means and the victim. It is His nature as King — this was Jesus' own gospel — to give, to forgive, to restore. "For God so loved the world that he gave his only Son . . . [to be] the expiation for our sins, and not for ours only but also for the sins of the whole world" (John 3:16; I John 2:2).

The Apostle Paul — and this is peculiarly his own contribution — had still another way of explaining the cross. Here, in addition to Romans 4:25 cited as the title to this section, these representative texts are important:

> Since all have sinned and fall short of the glory of God, they are justified by his grace as a gift, through the redemption which is in Christ Jesus (Rom. 3:23,24).

> Therefore, since we are justified by faith, we have peace with God through our Lord Jesus Christ (Rom. 5:1).

> We ourselves . . . know that a man is not justified by works of the law but through faith in Jesus Christ . . . (Gal. 2:15,16).

Justification by faith — this is the language of the law court. A criminal, a sinner is brought before the judge at the bar. He is obviously guilty; he even admits it. And then the judge gives the verdict: "Not guilty!"

Astounding, of course; but this is precisely the way Paul felt about his own conversion. Had he not, in fact, persecuted the tiny Christian sect: "For you have heard of my former life in Judaism, how I persecuted the church of God violently and tried to destroy it" (Gal. 1:13; cf. vs. 23; I Cor. 15:9)? Yet despite this, he, of all people the least deserving, had been swept off his feet by a sheer act of love, his new risen life in no sense merited, but an undeserved gift from above.

But why specifically the language of jurisprudence? There were several motivations. The Judaism of Paul's day sometimes tended to overstress the mechanical acts of religion — "works" —as a means whereby man could earn his salvation. The Apostle himself had followed this pattern ("extremely zealous was I for the traditions of my fathers"), and apparently been frustrated by it, even before his conversion sensing something fundamentally wrong (Gal. 1:14; Rom. 7:7–25). And when certain early Christians of Jewish background insisted that the praxis of Judaism be adopted by Gentile converts, meaning that they must undergo circumcision, and adhere to the ritualistic regulations which governed the lives of all good Jews, Paul replied in kind — legalism is not God's way for either Jew or Christian. When one gets down to essentials, man's salvation is a free gift; no matter what kind of works a man does, or how many, he merits nothing. The saved life is one which knows that all that life is and has results from the divine initiative. Not, then, by "doing" the Jewish law (or any law!) but by faith in Christ is God's way for man.

Paul has here penetrated to the heart of Jesus' own teaching and life. That man must cease being a god unto himself (or, in the Apostle's idiom, give up that pride of self-sufficiency which leads to the arrogant assumption that one can work his way to salvation) and accept life as God's gift, and his own dependence upon the Giver — this is precisely what Jesus' ministry was all about. And to have faith in Christ means to accept Christ's word that God, not man, is King, and the Christ life of death to all attempts at self-sufficiency. Not by self-striving, but by surrender, not by pointing to the good that one may have done, but by admission of guilt and by realization of one's need for the divine kingship — only in this way comes salvation. For no man can truly turn to God and remain the same as he was before. Not works, but the cross of total self-denial is what makes men new.

Paul's use of the language of the law court expresses this vividly. The sinner admits his guilt, yet God pronounces, "Not guilty!" This is indeed sheer gift! And yet, this imagery has been often misunderstood and misapplied. The trouble, of course, is that by every recognizable human standard, to pronounce "innocent" one who admits his guilt is to make nonsense of justice. And it raises questions: How can a just God act in this way? If God simply forgives, what is the reason or need for moral striving? Doubtless it is this problem which has induced Christians from time to time to proclaim an overly mechanistic interpretation of Christ's death as something which once and for all satisfied the demands of divine justice — the cross has paid the necessary penalty for sin which Everyman owes, it is because the scales have been redressed in this way that God can with justice say, "Not guilty!" [9]

It must be remembered, however, that Paul's legalistic

[9] New Testament writers have done this, too. The imagery which we noted on pp. 122–6 (and used by Paul himself) points in this direction. But it is important to remember that the early Christians were trying as best they could to explain an overpowering reality which actually defies precise categorization. The attempts of biblical writers do not represent a neatly thought out "Atonement theology," but are like many different shafts of light coming from here, there, and everywhere, each throwing a bit of light, each saying something important, each hinting at an aspect of the total truth. Even today many people have not yet resolved the problems which the questions posed in this paragraph raise. We should not, then, be overly critical of the earliest Christians because they failed to do so. One possible way of resolving the problems is suggested in the pages which immediately follow.

terminology is metaphorical. It hints at truth, but is not the whole truth. And that "whole truth" with respect to divine justice involves something which plays little part in the area of human legalistic endeavor — the fact that the relationship between God and His world is one of persons and of love.

But this points us to a last group of passages. These are of special importance, because they provide our best clue to what the Church's Atonement theology seeks to proclaim:

> For God so loved the world that he gave his only Son, that whoever believes in him should not perish but have eternal life (John 3:16).

> See what love the Father has given us, that we should be called children of God; and so we are (I John 3:1).

> . . . God's love has been poured into our hearts through the Holy Spirit which has been given to us (Rom. 5:5).

> . . . I live by faith in the Son of God, who loved me and gave himself for me (Gal. 2:20).

It is important to recall at this point two emphases of Jesus' teaching about God. In the first place, He is a Father. And so Jesus frequently uses the language of personal relationship — such words as forgiveness, joy, love, repentance — when he talks about God and His people.[10]

But also important is Jesus' understanding (and this is the biblical view generally) that God's relationship with His world is something dynamic. The King is no figurehead merely to be worshiped in His blue heaven. He actively reigns. And so it is, too, with the biblical concept of divine love which, ultimately, is not an emotion, but an activity, an "out-giving" of self. To say that God loves is a way of proclaiming that His is

[10] See above, pp. 23–5.

a Self-revealing "doing-things" relationship with His creation.[11] Divine love is a dynamic thrust which creates, reveals, proclaims, condemns, impels, re-creates.

This takes us directly to the heart of the Atonement. In Christ and his cross the believer encounters not simply an ideal toward which he must strive, but a power which re-creates. The Christ life of death to self in order to love is a dynamic which works change — to this the altered lives of the eyewitnesses testify. These lives avow, too, that one's own living of that Death-Resurrection life means not only freedom from the past, but also a joyous power through which the Christian can effect the salvation of others. And all this, because it is love which is involved, comes about only within the context of true personal relationship where legalism plays no role. That is, there is to God's justice a dimension which makes it quite unnecessary for us to try to defend Him with mechanical Atonement theories. The prodigal son, according to our limited human standards, deserved nothing; but he at last recognized his need — and the father forgave him, and he was restored (Luke 15:11–32). This is what love is, and what love does. To accept the cross for one's self is to acknowledge Christ as one's personal Savior, and his Father as the Sovereign of one's personal life in Christ. This is to be penetrated by forgiving love, for to welcome the cross means one's recognition of need, and so a lowering of the barrier of self and of self-sufficiency. In this way the new forgiven self begins, and is

---

[11] There is a close relationship here with the concept of the eternal Word of God (see above, pp. 77–85). It is significant that the Fourth Gospel, which specifically points to Christ as the Incarnation of that Word, especially stresses the sending of the Son as an act of divine love, and the attitude of the Father and the Son together toward the world as one of love. Love at root is a giving of self. This was the teaching and the life of the Jesus who so completely gave of himself for others. In him believers encountered the penetrating and effectual reality of God's love (see above, pp. 54–9), and understood him as God's gift of love to His world. The concept of the divine Word is a way of saying, as we have seen, that God's face is always turned *toward* His creation. Thus, we can see that the later Logos Christology is rooted in the observed event of the historical Jesus.

daily renewed by daily admission of need and dependence upon God.

We have a hint of all this in our own human experience of the love of person for person. Love is far more than emotion — it is a stubborn and persistent giving of one's self to and for the beloved, no matter what the hurt. And often enough we see it happen around us, so that we know it can always be this way — such stubborn love eventually penetrates: of his own free will the beloved says, "I'm sorry," and admits his need for the love which is given. And justice? — there is no talk of justice, nor necessity for it. The "I'm sorry" restores the broken relationship. Nor is there any fear that such free forgiveness will discourage moral striving. For there is nothing that the recipient of forgiveness desires more than to do the will of the one by whom he is so graciously and abundantly loved.[12]

This is reconciliation, this is At-one-ment, this is God's way with His world, and a hint as to why Calvary's cross is such an objective once-for-all reality in the Church's life. It does far more than inspire one "to be good." It is a dynamic which makes new people, now as well as in those first days when Jesus' followers said, "he died for our sins," and showed that this was true by the new manner of their lives.

X

And sitteth on the right hand
of God the Father Almighty

This affirmation comes down to us from the ground floor of the Church's origins. For the enthronement of Christ at God's right hand, or Session, as it is frequently called, was one of the earliest ways of proclaiming Jesus' Resurrection, and of under-

[12] See further below, pp. 214 f.

lining certain facets of its meaning.[1] In the chronological sequence of the Creed, of course, it is preceded by Descent into hell and Ascension. But in contrast to Session, these other concepts were not especially stressed in the early years of the Church's life.

Actually, we should note at this point, the full programmatic scheme of "events" (Crucifixion, Descent, Resurrection, Ascension, Session, Second Coming) was a late New Testament phenomenon. There was, following upon Jesus' death, one great overwhelming fact — God had raised him — which proved to be inexhaustible in its meaning. As time passed, attempts to understand more fully the significance of what God had done resulted in the affirmations of Descent, Ascension, Session, and Second Coming, all of which are vivid pictorial proclamations of the Resurrection. As the earliest of these, we shall consider Session first.

In a moment of confident enthusiasm, two of Jesus' disciples, the brothers James and John, approached him with a special request: "Grant us to sit, one at your right hand and one at your left, in your glory" (Mark 10:37). The immediate left and right were the positions of special honor, and particularly the latter. To the right of the throne sat the host's special guest, or he who more than any other shared the king's authority. The petition of James and John, then, was a self-seeking request for pre-eminent status when the Kingdom proclaimed by Jesus should arrive.

Again we note Psalm 110:1: "The Lord [God] says to my lord: *'Sit at my right hand,* till I make your enemies your footstool.'" Understood by Jesus' followers as Messianic prophecy, these words were used to hail the risen Christ as no less than

[1] See above, p. 106, fn. 9.

the wielder of God's authority.[2] To all intents and purposes, Psalm 110:1 has become a part of the Christian Creed.

Twice, according to the Gospel tradition, Jesus himself referred to this psalm. In one instance he appears to have suggested that the concept of a purely nationalistic Messiah held by many was inadequate.[3] David (who reputedly wrote the psalm) called the Messiah "Lord"; must he not, then, be much more than a human scion of David (Mark 12:35-37)? And then during the trial before the Sanhedrin Jesus states, "and you will see the Son of man sitting at the right hand of Power, and coming with the clouds of heaven" (Mark 14:62). The Son of Man was no human political leader, but a supernatural heavenly figure.[4] Mention of him here in conjunction with the reminiscence of Psalm 110 ("sitting at the right hand") underlines the vividness of Jesus' own Messianic expectation.

That Jesus was speaking of himself in these instances is dubious.[5] But there is no doubt as to what the first Christians believed. The following texts are typical:

> This Jesus God raised up, and of that we all are witnesses. Being therefore exalted at the right hand of God . . . (Acts 2:32,33).

> . . . Is it Christ Jesus, who died, yes, who was raised from the dead, who is at the right hand of God, who indeed intercedes for us (Rom. 8:34)?

> which he accomplished in Christ when he raised him from the dead and made him sit at his right hand in the heavenly places, far above all rule and authority and power and dominion, and above every name that is named, not only in this age but also in that which is to come; and he has put all things under his feet and has made him the

---

[2] See above, pp. 67–70. Italics mine.
[3] See above, p. 69.
[4] On Jesus as Son of Man, see below, pp. 143–53.
[5] See below, pp. 145–7, and particularly fn. 3.

head over all things for the church . . . (Eph. 1:20–22; cf. Phil. 2:9–11).

> But when Christ had offered for all time a single sacrifice for sins, he sat down at the right hand of God, then to wait until his enemies should be made a stool for his feet (Heb. 10:12,13; cf. I Cor. 15:24–28).

Each of these passages proclaims Christ as he who was "prophesied" in Psalm 110. We have already noted use of the title *Kyrios* as pointing to the post-Resurrection apprehension of Jesus' continuing personal authoritative Lordship over his followers.[6] But the last two texts just cited drastically broaden the scope of this authority. The Resurrection meant Christ's victory and subsequent rule over all the universe. His Lordship extends over the entire cosmos. Everything that is hostile to God, or to man as belonging to God, has been subdued.

It does not matter that in one instance (Ephesians) the victory is spoken of as complete, or that elsewhere (Hebrews and I Corinthians) it is viewed as yet to attain its fullness. The point is that what God has done in sending the Son penetrates into the heart of the entire universe. It has to do not simply with our little sphere of concrete phenomenal existence, but with the whole cosmos, the invisible and the unknown, as well as the visible and known. No matter what the human circumstance, the Christian's view of the world can only be at root optimistic. For he knows that God reigns, God is in control, and that to all things there is meaning and purpose. Christ sitting at God's right hand, Christ winning a victory over spirit powers — this, we are told, is "mythological" language. Of course it is; but was ever myth more meaningful than this?

But there is still another dimension. At this point it will be helpful to turn back to pages 79 f. where we cited the following texts: I Corinthians 8:6; Colossians 1:15–17; Hebrews

[6] See above, pp. 64–70.

1:1-4; John 1:1-4,14. Only in the third of these is Psalm 110:1 specifically alluded to, but the affinity between all four is self-evident.

In these passages Christ is proclaimed not only as the victor and henceforth ruler, but as the actual principle of the entire creative process. Before the worlds were, he was. It was through him that all created things came into existence, in him that all things have their life and meaning and final purpose.

In short, it was not long before this psalm, which had been used by the first believers as a Messianic confession of faith, became a vehicle for the expression of the most exalted Christology to which the New Testament Church attained. We need but repeat what was asserted at an earlier point: "It was through His Word — which as Word of command is powerful to initiate and to bring to completion, and as intelligible Word reveals and can be known — that God creates, gives and sustains life, delivers, re-creates, brings all existence and history to their fulfillment." [7] Such was Jesus Christ!

We have already hinted at the importance of the all-conquering, all-sustaining cosmic Christ as a theological concept.[8] But does Logos Christology have any immediate and personal meaning for Christian believers?

For one thing, it gives us a clue with regard to man's deepest queries with respect to the world in which he lives. Who is God? Why did He create the universe, and with what end in view? What is His continuing relationship with the world? The fact that He exists — what does this mean for the people who inhabit the world?

There are no easy answers to such basic questions as these. But cosmic Christology says that one must start in his search by recognizing that the human Jesus of Nazareth is at the same time the focal point of God's revelation of all that He is and

[7] See above, pp. 81 f.
[8] See above, pp. 77–85.

does. What God was, the eternal Word was. And in Jesus Christ that Word manifested himself in our midst. That is, Christ is what the world is all about, the key to the whole, its beginning, its continuance, its end.

Beyond this we can perhaps go a step further. It was love as a creative and re-creative power which the first Christians believed they had encountered in the self-sacrificing life of Jesus. And it was something so central in their lives that they became convinced that here in fact was that which God is and does always and everywhere. Love, that is, is one manner, perhaps the least inadequate manner, of describing God's way with His universe. Here, in brief, is the fundamental principle of creation and of coherence.

Or take the Death-Resurrection pattern of Christ's life and of the believer's life. This, too, is now proclaimed as cosmic principle. If love is God's way with the world, that which is the essence of love, death to self, is God's way *for* the world, and the means by which all things come to that fulfillment which is the divinely willed End.

The history of species or civilizations or social movements, even, gives a hint — that there must be sacrifice on the part of one or many if there is to be gain. And again speaking in general terms, we see this principle in the growth and development of individuals, because self-denial for a greater good is an essential part of growth towards physical and mental maturity. But it is the Christian frame of reference in which the principle shines most clearly. Salvation for each person is a finishing of that creation which was begun at his birth. It is only by death to the wrong kind of self, and the consequent beginning of a new life in Christ, that one can become the full person which he was born to be.[9]

[9] Note below, especially pp. 164–9, and throughout the discussion of the third Article, the reiterated thesis that it is in relationship with one's neighbor that God is known, and that only so is salvation possible. True life is to be "in Christ," which is to love. Here is a further striking example of love as a fundamental principle of God's creation.

"And sitteth on the right hand of God the Father Almighty" — the life, death, Resurrection of Jesus Christ is the answer to everything that man wants or needs to know.

XI

He descended into hell

Jesus spent the period between Crucifixion and Resurrection in the place of departed spirits. The writings of such second century figures as Ignatius, Polycarp and Irenaeus show that this affirmation soon became a commonplace of Christian thinking. In New Testament times, however, it played a minor role.

The word "hell" today is woefully misleading. It has over the centuries acquired lurid connotations which are thoroughly un-Christian. It is well to remember that the biblical concept, although by no means free from such crudities, has its root in the more general concept of Hades, that shadowy underworld region which is the abode of the dead. The more recent translations of the New Testament, for example the Revised Standard Version and the New English Bible, have in most texts substituted "Hades" for "hell" — and properly so.[1]

Pre-Christian Jewish speculation as to life after death was complex. Hades roughly corresponded to the *Sheol* of primitive Semitic thought, and to the subterranean abode of the dead in Greek mythology. There dwelt the departed in an existence bereft of either pain or pleasure. In the centuries immediately preceding the Christian era, probably under the influence of

[1] In the Prayer Book of the Episcopal Church there is a rubric which permits substitution of the words, "He went into the place of departed spirits" for "He descended into hell" when the Apostles' Creed is recited (see, for example, p. 15). Congregations seldom avail themselves of this permission.

Iranian thought, there developed the idea of a separate place of torture (Gehenna) for the wicked. The return of the departed from Hades to a meaningful existence, namely, resurrection of the body, is also a late development. It was out of this general background that the later traditional pattern of bodily resurrection for final judgment and consignment to heaven, or to hell as a place of torment, emerged.

Jesus upon occasion used such vivid imagery. In his story of Dives and Lazarus, the latter is comforted, but the rich man suffers burning torments (Luke 16:19–31). This admonition, too, comes to mind: "And if your hand causes you to sin, cut it off; it is better for you to enter life maimed than with two hands to go to hell [Gehenna], to the unquenchable fire" (Mark 9:43; cf. Matt. 5:27–30).

Such sayings as these, however, must be viewed in proper context. In the first place, we have here typical examples of Semitic hyperbole, dramatic underlining in order to drive one's point home. Such hyperbole, whether it be a conscious or unconscious device, demands a realistic interpretation.

Over and beyond this, however, one must ask if insistence upon the literalness of Jesus' punishment language does not lead one into irreconcilable conflict with his own teaching about the nature of God as one who loves and forgives. We have earlier proposed that God's love demands nothing, and wishes nothing but welcoming acceptance of love, and that because this is true, the mechanical concept of so much sin, so much wrath, so much punishment, so many amends, is, at best, a dubious way to understand the Father of Jesus Christ.[2]

What, then, are we to say to the references to hell — and there are several — in the recorded words of Jesus?[3] Is it sufficient simply to dismiss them as hyperbole? They must be taken far more seriously than that. There is not the slightest doubt

[2] See above, pp. 128–31.
[3] See Mark 9:43–48 (cf. Matt. 18:8–9); Luke 12:5 (cf. Matt. 10:28); Matt. 5:22; 23:15; Matt. 11:23 (cf. Luke 10:15); Luke 16:23.

that Jesus took a most grave view of sin. This is apparent not only from the texts already cited above, but also from his frequent warnings of judgment, and his repeated urgings to repentance. That man cannot disobey God with impunity was an integral part of his gospel. Traditionally, and rightly, this has been taken to mean that, in some form at least, there is such a thing as divine punishment — and committed Christians are only too well aware of this. They know through their own attempts and failures that to go contrary to the demands of love is to be miserably out of harmony with both man and God.

But we may well wonder about the extremist position that claims that there is a divine punishment which goes on forever and ever in an unremitting blazing hell. Can one really speak of dominical authority for such a view? For the Jesus of history who lies behind the New Testament witness was a man of his own times who used the thought forms of those times — and, again, this is to recall the idiom of dramatic hyperbole. Moreover, he was a near-Eastern Semite, and as such had neither the set of mind nor the passion which characterizes our Western culture for logically ordering all his insights in neat and perfectly consistent schema. He deeply understood that it is God's nature to love, and to search for that which is lost until it is found. He was equally aware that rejection of God is a tragic matter with inevitable consequences — and in the language of his day he avowed this, too. And there he left it.

But is not the paradox here more seeming than real? If, indeed, God's love is a divine power of omnipotent deity which forgives and re-creates, then surely the resolution of this apparent contradiction is not too difficult. The hard core reality of the biblical punishment language is an undeniable fact of Christian experience. But we may hesitate to claim that such imagery represents the ultimate destiny of any individual whom God has created.[4]

Turning now to the credal phrase, the New Testament has

[4] See below, pp. 214 f.

only two texts indubitably relevant to the Descent into Hades:

> For Christ . . . made alive in the spirit ' . . . went and preached to the spirits in prison, who formerly did not obey, when God's patience waited in the days of Noah . . . (I Pt. 3:18–20).

> For this is why the gospel was preached even to the dead, that though judged in the flesh like men, they might live in the spirit like God (I Pt. 4:6).

The central witness is clear — that those who had lived and died before Jesus' time also received the good news of salvation. It may be that Matthew 12:40 and Ephesians 4:9 f. are also references of Church tradition to the Descent. That Romans 10:7 has this in view is highly improbable. Paul seems to have known nothing of such a phenomenon, and it is a concept which may well have arisen after his day. That the historical Jesus predicted such a post-Crucifixion ministry for himself is highly improbable.

The Descent into Hades illustrates with special clarity the fact that "myth" rightly understood must not be equated with falsity, but is rather one of the media by which truth is proclaimed and apprehended. The real significance of this credal phrase is its affirmation that the event of Jesus Christ had crucial meaning for all creation for all time. This is to underline again the vividness and inexhaustible significance of the Resurrection faith. More specifically, the Descent spells out that cosmic Christology which we have outlined in previous sections. And when we recall the non-scientific world view of people in that day, we recognize that there is no redundancy here.

Most people pictured our world as a three-story universe. The fact that the life, death, and Resurrection of Jesus was a cosmic event inevitably led to the picture of his salvation work in "geographical" terms. He visited every corner of the universe. No person ever escapes the Creator's dominion, or the possibility of becoming that which he was born to be. "O death, where is thy victory? O death, where is they sting?" (I Cor. 15:55). This is as true for those who lived before Jesus of Nazareth as for those who come after.

" . . . Fear not, I am the first and the last, and the living one; I died, and behold I am alive for evermore, and I have the keys of Death and Hades" (Rev. 1:17,18). Christ is all in all!

XII

He ascended into heaven

For the space of forty days the risen Jesus continued to appear to his disciples instructing them in the things pertaining to the Kingdom of God. And then, "as they were looking on, he was lifted up, and a cloud took him out of their sight" (Acts 1:1-11). As the prophet Elijah who was carried up by a whirlwind, Jesus was bodily assumed in order that he might take his place and commence his reign at God's right hand (II Kings 2:11). The same author, Luke, at the end of his Gospel recounts that "While he blessed them, he parted from them, and [some manuscripts add] was carried up into heaven" (Luke 24:51). John apparently knew this tradition, perhaps Matthew as well (John 20:17; Matt. 28:16,17). The original Gospel of Mark makes no mention of it.[1]

There is some variation of details. Luke's Gospel locates the Ascension at Bethany, a village about one and a half miles east of Jerusalem, and the event occurred on the same day as the

[1] Mark 16:19, which is part of that addition to the original Gospel which commences with vs. 9, reads, "So then the Lord Jesus, after he had spoken to them, was taken up into heaven, and sat down at the right hand of God."

Resurrection (24:50, cf. 23:43; John 20:17). But in his second volume he notes that there was a forty-day period of appearances prior to the Ascension, and more specifically he locates the event at Mount Olivet, on the side of which the village of Bethany stood. Neither Matthew nor John, nor the late addition to Mark's Gospel, mentions any forty-day interval.

Elsewhere there are hints, but little more, of this tradition. One passage in I Peter is of special interest because it is the only place in the entire New Testament which appears to include the complete programming of the Resurrection event as we find it in the Creed: "For Christ also *died for sins* once for all . . . but made alive in the spirit; in which he *went and preached to the spirits in prison* . . . through the *resurrection* of Jesus Christ, who has *gone into heaven* [bodily ascension?] and is *at the right hand of God,* with angels, authorities, and powers subject to him" (3:18-22, italics mine).

Other Ascension references are more dubious. In Ephesians 4:8–10 we have a rhetorical balancing of descent and ascent — but the meaning of this text is as doubtful as is its genuine Pauline authorship. In I Timothy 3:16 there is the cryptic statement that Jesus was "taken up in glory." Hebrews speaks of him as one who "has passed through the heavens" (4:14). These last, however, may all be more general references to Jesus' Resurrection. There is no evidence that the writers were thinking of a literal levitation phenomenon. The same is true of Peter's speeches in Acts, where the risen Christ's heavenly status is described in such nonspecific terms as "glorification" and "exaltation." [2] The Gospels give no hint that Jesus predicted any such event. Finally, our earliest written witness to the faith of the first believers, the epistles of Paul, shows no knowledge of such a happening.

The Apostolic Witness, then, in its earliest form does not proclaim an Ascension into heaven. Like the Descent into

[2] See above, p. 104, fn. 5, p. 105, fn. 6, and p. 106, fn. 9.

Hades, this event was not underlined as of special importance during the first Christian century. And we may well surmise that the ground root of this credal affirmation is one of the Resurrection appearances of Jesus told in such a way as to explain the gradual lessening of that peculiar vividness which initially characterized believers' discernment of the risen one. The ascension motif was prominent in popular Judaism, as is evidenced especially by tales of such translations of Old Testament worthies told in non-canonical Jewish literature. So Jesus was taken up to the highest level of the universe. In this manner his immediate earthly ministry came to a close. Now he commences his glorious and all-powerful reign enthroned at God's right hand, having, as it were, cleared the pathway which his own will follow: "In my Father's house are many rooms; if it were not so, would I have told you that I go to prepare a place for you?" (John 14:2).

The Ascension thus proclaims Christ's role as king of all creation. It underlines, moreover, the goal and the glory which are the ultimate reason for man's existence, and which, "in Christ," are possible. These truths of the Apostolic Witness do not in any way stand or fall with the literal historicity of Descent and Ascension. The particular form of the affirmations was an inevitable result of the world picture of the day.

XIII

From thence he shall come
to judge the quick and the dead

Joyfully Jesus' followers proclaimed him as King Messiah reigning triumphant over all the powers of evil. The decisive victory had been won; the end of all things, especially the end of sorrow and tribulation and death, was at hand. True, there had been a delay — but no matter. Soon they would share in the glories of an utterly "new heaven and new earth."

And how would this all come about? In his second volume, Luke describes it with vivid literalness:

> Men of Galilee, why do you stand looking into heaven? This Jesus, who was taken up from you into heaven, will come in the same way as you saw him go into heaven (Acts 1:11).

There was no doubt of the final outcome. He who had promised had at last sent His Messiah, and was powerful to accomplish that which He had begun.

The concept of the Parousia, to use the technical term for Jesus' return, has borrowed heavily from pre-Christian Judaism. At the same time, Jewish Messianism did not contemplate a double visitation by God's vicegerent. We must go back a bit.

In one of its many forms, Israel's future hope anticipated the coming of God's Kingdom as radically altering the present world.[1] This cataclysmic event was pictured as a time of bloody battles between the hosts of God (sometimes led by the Messiah) and the hosts of Satan, holocausts of fire and brimstone, plague and pestilence, the opening of the graves of the dead, woes, terror, judgment. Judaism borrowed many of these details from the world view and imagery of Iranian and Babylonian mythology. And the whole reflects a certain pessimism induced by centuries of national insecurity and frustration. The world had become so evil, that only radical divine action, something utterly new, would avail. The sure faith that God could

[1] See above, p. 39.

144

and would act was still there, but for many the more idyllic nationalistic future hope did not suffice. History, as presently known and experienced, would end.

This conviction also shaped the Messianic hope. Here, too, there was borrowing from other mythologies. Messiah would be not simply a scion of David, an ideal but human king. Rather, corresponding to the stupendousness of his task as God's vicegerent, he would be a supernatural figure, the Son of Man. Presently living in heaven, he would at the decisive moment appear, perhaps borne to earth on the clouds of the sky, accompanied by hosts of angels, to make war against the powers of Satan, raise the dead, give judgment in God's name, and henceforth rule victoriously and eternally over a new heaven and a new earth.

Jesus appears not to have indulged to any great extent in the more bizarre aspects of this kind of speculation.[2] His own frequent use of the title Son of Man, however, indicates that he was familiar with this accent. The following texts show us his understanding of this enigmatic figure:

> For whoever is ashamed of me and of my words in this adulterous and sinful generation, of him will the Son of man also be ashamed, when he comes in the glory of his Father with the holy angels (Mark 8:38).

> And I tell you, every one who acknowledges me before men, the Son of man also will acknowledge before the angels of God; but he who denies me before men will be denied before the angels of God (Luke 12:8,9).

Here Jesus points to the Son of Man as one other than

[2] Mark 13, and its parallels in Matthew and Luke, is a typical example of later Christian apocalyptic taken over from Judaism. Jesus believed in the coming of the Kingdom as concrete temporal event. But his own cautious view is better represented by the following saying: "Take heed, watch and pray; for you do not know when the time will come" (Mark 13:32,33; cf. I Th. 5:2).

himself.[3] And the significance of his reference to this awesome heavenly figure is clear in the light of that radical crisis future hope — condemnation and blessing in the context of a cataclysmic creation of a new world — which we outlined as the view held by many in his day. Jesus' gospel was a crisis proclamation, the announcement, that is, of something crucial for the world of men — that God is King, that people must let Him reign, that He will reign. The picture of a gentle figure

[3] Not all will concur with this judgment. Jesus' use of this title remains somewhat of an enigma. The evidence permits more than one interpretation.

The title appears in the Gospels frequently, and always on the lips of Jesus himself. That he did often use it seems indubitable. Taken by themselves, Mark 8:38 and Luke 12:8,9 (just cited), are most naturally understood as references to the Son of Man as one other than the speaker. In addition, there are numerous other ambiguous texts (for example, Mark 13:26; Luke 12:40; 18:8; Matt. 10:23; 16:28; etc.) which can be similarly understood. There is also a third category of texts in which Jesus appears specifically to claim to be the Son of Man (for example, Mark 8:31; 9:12,31; Mark 10:33; Matt. 26:2; Luke 7:34; 9:58; 17:25; etc.). In the light of these, the second category just mentioned could be taken as Jesus' reference to himself, and possibly even Mark 8:38 and Luke 12:8,9.

Many, however, are of the opinion that the simplest explanation in this case is the best one, viz., in Mark 8:38 and Luke 12:8,9, we have evidence, all but covered over by later Church tradition, that Jesus did not make this identification. The texts which appear to contradict this reflect the view of the post-Resurrection Church. Here, i.e., is a phenomenon parallel to that which occurred with respect to the titles Christ, and Son of God as a divine claim. Jesus did not make for himself the status claims implied by these titles. The Church, in the light of her total experience, did this for him, thereby using these titles as confessions of faith.

As to the whole matter of the historical Jesus' Messianic and divine consciousness, the following question is relevant. Would genuine humanity, which, as taught and lived by Jesus, has as its primary condition the welcome acceptance of its creatureliness and complete emptying of self (this was Jesus' gospel: "Let *God* reign!"), claim for itself unique status (as Messiah, or supernatural Son of Man, or divine Son of God)? To be recalled here is the discussion of Mark 10:17 f. on pp. 66 f. above. One wonders if such claims for self would not go against the very grain of Jesus' entire life and understanding of God. On the other hand, relevant to this whole problem is the tradition of Hebrew prophecy, and the matter of prophetic consciousness; the prophets *did* claim divine inspiration, and in this sense a status of special closeness to God.

Many, therefore, conclude that Jesus did identify himself with the Son of Man figure, his heavenly glory hidden during the earthly ministry, but soon to be revealed when the historical ministry was concluded. This view does not substantially change the course of the argument presented above.

seated quietly with children in his arms and ambling about the Galilean countryside is thoroughly misleading. His brief ministry was characterized by urgency, imperative demand, haste (Luke 10:1–16; 12:40; Matt. 16:28). Hurry and repent — the Kingdom is "awe-full," and comes at any moment as a thief in the night.

This is the atmosphere, the crisis atmosphere, of the Son of Man Messianism. The Kingdom is imperious reality, the Son of Man is coming — in this way, and because of its vividness, Jesus used a spectacular imagery to underline the "world-shaking" importance of God's sovereignty.

Jesus, raised by God and reigning in heaven, is himself the Son of Man. So the first Christians hailed him. What did it mean to make this affirmation? For one thing, it was yet another way of confessing him as the expected Jewish Messiah. More than this, however, there were particular circumstances which gave to this title a special role of its own.

The two texts cited on p. 145 make clear one reason for the Church's early identification of Jesus with the Son of Man. He himself understood his mission to be integrally related to the advent of God's Kingdom. An individual's readiness for the great event is contingent upon acceptance of Jesus' words of warning and promise. And his followers, both before and after the Good Friday weekend, had encountered in him more than just exhortation. To know him was to be penetrated by that very condemnation and blessing which the coming of the Son of Man was expected to bring.[4]

We can, however, be more specific. Jesus, although knowing that something of the reality of God's sovereignty was actually, through his own ministry, penetrating into people's lives, nevertheless heralded the fullness of the Kingdom as yet to come.

[4] See above, pp. 54–9.

Early believers, too, for all the vividness of their present experience, lived in anticipation, knew that the final outcome of God's action in Christ lay ahead. And it was this sure hope, in particular, which their use of the title Son of Man avowed.

It is not difficult to understand how this came about. During the first few weeks, or even months, Jesus' followers, in all probability, did not think specifically in terms of his return to earth. Excitement and expectation were the prevailing mood. Momentarily, they were convinced, the new creation which his life and death and Resurrection heralded would burst in upon them. But, as time passed, and as the old world and its problems continued, the Parousia hope, with its picture of Jesus returning on the clouds of heaven, came to the fore. And it speaks eloquently to the intensity of early Christian faith. The delay, really, was no matter. That which had happened to their lives was so irresistibly real, that no circumstances could override it; they knew that what God had begun, He would complete. In particular, however, it was because of Jesus — his teaching, his life, his Resurrection, his messiahship — that their feet had been set on a new path. Specifically, then, it was in terms of him that they saw the future. Surely, what *he* had begun *he,* as the risen Christ, was powerful to bring to completion. And so, dramatically and effectively, believers expressed their sure hope by saying that Jesus, as the Son of Man, would himself soon return with the fullness of the Kingdom.[5]

Turn the pages of the New Testament, however, and one notes that, apart from our four Gospels, only once (Acts 7:56) is Jesus given the specific title. We can only guess the reason for this. It may be that here is a phenomenon somewhat similar to that noted in connection with the title Christ — the peculiar "Jewishness" of the phrase Son of Man making it of limited usefulness for the Christian of Gentile upbringing.[6]

[5] To see this in its complete context, one must recall the association of this Messianic title in current Judaism with the denouement of the Kingdom, Jesus' own use of Son of Man as a means of heralding the future, and the certainty of believers after the Resurrection that he was in fact the Messiah.
[6] See above, pp. 62 f.

For that which it proclaimed — the sure return of Jesus as judge and savior — became at an early date one of the pivots of the Christian proclamation. In the following texts, for example, the precise title Son of Man does not appear, but that Jesus is being so described is apparent:

> and to wait for his Son from heaven, whom he raised from the dead, Jesus who delivers us from the wrath to come . . . (I Th. 1:10).

> For the Lord himself will descend from heaven with a cry of command, with the archangel's call, and with the sound of the trumpet of God. And the dead in Christ will rise first; then we who are alive, who are left, shall be caught up together with them in the clouds to meet the Lord in the air; and so we shall always be with the Lord (I Th. 4:16,17).

Already by the time of Paul's active missionary career, death for sin, Resurrection to Lordship, and Parousia had become the three fundamental tenets of the Church's gospel.

Let us sample a few other texts which express the Parousia hope:

> so that you are not lacking in any spiritual gift, as you wait for the revealing of our Lord Jesus Christ; who will sustain you to the end, guiltless in the day of our Lord Jesus Christ (I Cor. 1:7,8).

> so that you may approve what is excellent, and may be pure and blameless for the day of Christ (Phil. 1:10).

> and to grant rest with us to you who are afflicted, when the Lord Jesus is revealed from heaven with his mighty angels in flaming fire, inflicting vengeance upon those who do not know God and upon those who do not obey the gospel of our Lord Jesus. They shall suffer the punishment of eternal destruction and exclusion from the presence of the Lord and

from the glory of his might, when he comes on that day to be glorified in his saints . . . (II Th. 1:7-10).

In such words as these we see how heavily the primitive Church borrowed from Judaism. The references to revelation and "day of Christ," as well as the vividness of the language, bring to mind a complex of ideas associated with Old Testament pictures of "the day of the Lord," that final moment when God as King would manifest His full power and glory. Often, as we have seen, that day was pictured as ushering in catastrophic upheavals of the kind which in later times came to be associated with the Hebraic Son of Man Messianism. And Christians simply took over this imagery, and applied it to Messiah Jesus. The cataclysmic "day" will be that of Christ's Parousia when the full glory, which was hidden during the earthly ministry, will be revealed. The Kingdom, which is now in his hands, will soon have full sway throughout the whole world. God through His Messiah will at last be all in all. In short, this is Son of Man Christology.

Another phenomenon closely associated with the Jewish future hope was the resurrection of the dead. Ultimately, of course, it was because of Jesus' Resurrection that his followers looked forward to their own. But in describing this event, they borrowed heavily from Judaism's picture of the events which were a part of the Son of Man's coming. This we shall discuss more fully in connection with the third Article.[7]

Still another category of thought closely connected with Hebraic use of this title concerned the last judgment. These Christian texts are typical (italics mine):

And he commanded us to preach to the people, and to testify that he is the one ordained by God to be *judge of the living and the dead* (Acts 10:42).

I charge you in the presence of God and of Christ Jesus

[7] See below, pp. 202–9.

150

who is *to judge the living and the dead,* and by his appearing and his kingdom (II Tim. 4:1).

For we must all appear before the judgment seat of Christ, so that each one may receive good or evil, according to what he has done in the body (II Cor. 5:10).

When the Son of man comes in his glory, and all the angels with him, then he will sit on his glorious throne. Before him will be gathered all the nations, and he will separate them one from another as a shepherd separates the sheep from the goats, and he will place the sheep at his right hand, but the goats at the left (Matt. 25:31–33).

The similarity between the first two of these texts and the credal "from thence he shall come to judge the quick [living] and the dead" is striking.

In earlier Old Testament parlance, it is God Himself who is spoken of as Judge. Later Judaism often attributed this function to the heavenly Son of Man. Now, however, the role of judge becomes the prerogative of Christ. The Fourth Gospel puts it this way: "The Father judges no one, but has given all judgment to the Son, that all may honor the Son (5:22).[8]

The ultimate reason for this transference of function lies in the teaching and life of Jesus himself. He had proclaimed that to deny God's sovereignty is to go against the very grain of the universe. Furthermore, his words and life had both made clear the ethical implications of that sovereignty, and made real to people the condemnation or blessing which results from rejection or acceptance of the divine kingship. And then, as we have seen, he had said that readiness for the coming of the Son of Man depended upon one's reaction to his own gospel.[9]

In short, in every way, he, Jesus, had become for Christians

---

[8] Transitions of this sort did not take place all at once. Note (in contrast to II Cor. 5:10 above) Rom. 14:10: "For we shall all stand before the judgment seat of *God"!*
[9] See above, pp. 55 f and 147.

the criterion and mediator of judgment. He it was who would determine the fate of all things when God's End should arrive.

Frequently in the New Testament the picture of Jesus' Parousia, and of the last things, is couched in language which is as bizarre as anything to be found in pre-Christian Judaism. Particularly, one thinks of Mark 13, II Thessalonians 1,2, and, above all, Revelation, a book whose imagery, in some places, is not only crude, but downright cruel. The early Church in this respect appears to have gone much further than did Jesus himself. Is not, perhaps, his own greater reticence significant of a less literalistic and deeper understanding?

Primitive Christianity's excesses, however, should not surprise us. For all the newness of their lives, the first believers remained people — and people of their own times. Their motives were mixed, their understanding but partial. After all, the Church even today is struggling to comprehend and apply the full implications of her gospel. Nor, many Christians currently hold, is there need to insist that Jesus will literally and physically return to earth on the clouds of heaven, or that God's completion of the creative process will involve a holocaust of misery and woe. And yet, for all this, and understand the details how one will, the Parousia concept remains an essential part of the Christian faith.

It proclaims, for one thing, that to let God reign over what is His own is something which not only should be, but will be — whether one desires it this way or not. For the world at large, or for individual lives, to deny His sovereignty cannot but have consequences, and this not because God is a vindictive despot, but simply because His way is *the* way of all creation, and any contrary way makes for inevitable disharmony and malaise. The world, however, does not walk in darkness. The divine will can be known in Jesus the Christ. And again, whether one desires it or not, judgment and condemnation and blessing in Christ and by Christ are an integral part of human existence. For in Jesus of Nazareth is to be seen not just an isolated, though deeply meaningful, event, but that fundamental principle of creation and existence around which the universe coheres.[10] But chiefly, the Parousia means that the divine triumph is not the victory of arbitrary power, but of forgiveness and love; for of these things also Christ was, and remains, the incarnation. For the one who so desires it, his "coming again" can be sheer joy.

The Parousia also proclaims this — that God's purposes are sure, God's hand is powerful to accomplish, His will *will* be done and, even when it seems least likely, is being done. Here one recalls the Hebraic concept of history as an arrow moving towards a goal.[11] We do not suggest that other "philosophies" of history are without value. The whole truth requires many perspectives. But the Hebraic-Christian view (the Parousia proclaims God's End!) underlines this all-important good news — that God has a purpose, which means that all life has a purpose, and that no individual life is without meaning, and that God is powerful not only to create, but to re-create, which is to say that no individual life is without hope.

The Christian believes that God's purpose for him, and power to perform the same, are revealed and given through Christ. And to proclaim his Parousia is to affirm this — that the words of Jesus of Nazareth are true words, and that what God did in and through him can work a glorious fulfillment unto salvation in each individual who wills it.

[10] See above, pp. 77–84, and 133–7.
[11] See above, pp. 38–40.

III

ARTICLE THREE

I believe in the Holy Ghost:
The Holy Catholic Church;
The Communion of Saints:
The Forgiveness of sins:
The Resurrection of the body:
And the Life everlasting. Amen.

I

Introduction

A few days after the Ascension some of Jesus' followers "were
all together in one place." Their purpose apparently was to
observe a major event of the Jewish liturgical calendar, the
Feast of Weeks, or Pentecost. What happened is best described
in Luke's own words:

> And suddenly a sound came from heaven like the rush of
> a mighty wind, and it filled all the house where they were
> sitting. And there appeared to them tongues as of fire,
> distributed and resting on each one of them. And they·
> were all filled with the Holy Spirit and began to speak in
> other tongues, as the Spirit gave them utterance (Acts
> 2:2-4).

This occurrence the participants understood as no less than a
seizure by the very power of God Himself. Actually, Luke's
account dramatizes something which was a repeated experience
of early Christian assemblies. On another occasion, for example,
"when they had prayed, the place in which they were gathered
together was shaken; and they were all filled with the Holy
Spirit and spoke the word of God with boldness" (Acts 4:31).[1]

[1] A reading of I Cor. 14 gives a good insight into the character of the early
Christian gatherings.

There was nothing more characteristic of the earliest Church than such awareness of the Spirit.

Let us return to the Pentecostal event. So startling were its outward manifestations that some mocked: "[These people] are filled with new wine" (2:13). But, No, replied Peter, "these men are not drunk, as you suppose, since it is only the third hour of the day" (vs. 15). And then in his first speech he proceeds to explain that the crucified one is the long-awaited Messiah now in heaven, and that "having received from the Father the promise of the Holy Spirit, he has poured out this which you see and hear" (vs. 33). "What," the listeners then ask, "shall we do?" "Repent," Peter answers, "and be baptized every one of you in the name of Jesus Christ for the forgiveness of your sins; and you shall receive the gift of the Holy Spirit" (vss. 37,38). Henceforth, this was to be God's way unto salvation.

Here in sum is the shape of the tripartite Creed. The first Article proclaims God, the second His Son, and the third the Holy Spirit which dominates the lives of those who respond to the preaching of God and Christ. This is precisely the pattern of Luke's account in the second chapter of Acts. Jesus is God's Messiah. To know and to welcome this is new life "in the Spirit." The Christian task is to proclaim the one God and His Christ. To accept this good news is to join with those who know the power of transformed lives.[2]

More than this, however, Peter in his exhortation speaks of repentance and baptism. And although implicit rather than explicit in this first sermon, acceptance of God and His Messiah means membership in a new community, the Church. Actually, as we shall see, Peter's sermon contains all the basic elements of our third Article. Life in the Spirit is life in the Church. And it is a new saved life, begun with forgiveness for the past at baptism, continuing with new power for every present moment,

[2] This same pattern underlies all the Petrine speeches in Acts.

and with a sure hope for the future. In short, here in outline form is the remainder of our study:

The Holy Spirit

The Church

Baptism for the Forgiveness of Sins — Salvation as Past Event

The Church as Holy, Catholic, Communion of Saints — Salvation Through Striving

Resurrection of the Body, Life Everlasting — Salvation as Future

One final introductory note: the Christian today confesses the Holy Spirit as an article of faith. But in earliest times, Spirit, Church, Salvation were not primarily matters of intellectual assent or of confessional recital, but things that happened. Speaking in terms of credal origins, one might put it this way — the first and second Articles affirm what the earliest Christians themselves confessed and proclaimed; the third Article tells us what resulted when that gospel was accepted.

In what follows, then, we shall be seeing something of the actual impact of the things that happened "under Pontius Pilate" upon real people who were in all essentials very much like ourselves.

II

The Holy Spirit

The phrase "Holy Ghost," which is frequently used in liturgies as well as in our two Creeds, is today an enigma to many. Even "Holy Spirit" fails, at least in our day, to convey the full meaning that it had for early Christians. We must look at the biblical usage.

In the Old Testament, "Spirit of God" has a wide range of meaning. But whether the reference is to divine creativity, or to the power of leadership, or to prophetic inspiration, always the basic thrust is that of activity, getting things done.[1] We say that "God is spirit" (John 4:24). Here we are speaking of His nature; He is immaterial, invisible. But this does not mean that He is aloof, withdrawn in a kind of lofty inactivity. In Hebrew the word for "spirit" is the same as that for "air on the move," or "wind." And the chief aspect of this term as applied to God in the Bible is that of powerful accomplishment. So through His Spirit God creates, commands, governs, inspires, redeems.[2] The Spirit, we might say, is one of the ways in which God is Lord of history, one of the ways in which He reigns as King.

Of particular importance is the connection with Israel's future hope. Isaiah, for example, says that the Spirit will be "poured upon us from on high, and the wilderness [become] a fruitful

[1] See, for example, Gen. 1:2, Jdgs. 3:10, 11:29, I Sam. 11:6, 16:13, II Sam. 23:2, Is. 48:16.
[2] Here one inevitably thinks of the earlier descriptions of God as love (see p. 130, fn. 11), and of the divine Word (pp. 77–85). Each of these represents a somewhat different accent with respect to the divine activity. It is not surprising that these concepts tend to overlap, for all three are impelled by the same basic conviction that it is the nature of God to be actively engaged with His creation.

160

field, and the fruitful field [be] deemed a forest" (32:15).[3] Far
more dramatic, however, is this representative text:

> And it shall come to pass afterward,
>> that I will pour out my spirit on all flesh;
> your sons and your daughters shall prophesy,
>> your old men shall dream dreams,
>> and your young men shall see visions.
> Even upon the menservants and maidservants
>> in those days, I will pour out my spirit.

> And I will give portents in the heavens and on the
> earth . . . before the great and terrible day of the Lord
> comes (Joel 2:28–31).

The new age, whenever and however it might come, would be
heralded by a startling increase in manifest divine activity —
God as King at last reigning irresistibly. And significantly, it is
this same text from Joel which Peter cites as explanation of the
Pentecostal charismatic experience (Acts 2:16–21). God's decisive moment in history has dawned! But all this, of course, was
because Messiah had come. Again we must look at the Old
Testament background.

Israel's prophets and kings were believed to be especially
endowed with power from God. When anointed for kingship
by Samuel, "the Spirit of the Lord came mightily upon David
from that day forward" and, significantly, departed from
Saul his predecessor (I Sam. 16:13 f.). As immediate representative of God, the earthly king was divinely empowered for his
task: "I have found David, my servant; with my holy oil I
have anointed him; so that my hand shall ever abide with
him, my arm also shall strengthen him" (Ps. 89:20,21).

So, too, the Messiah, the future ruler of God's Kingdom,
would be, in a very special way, a channel of divine activity,
and receive special strengthening. "The Spirit of the Lord shall

---

[3] See also Ez: 11:19; 36:26; 37:14; 39:29; Is. 44:3; etc.

rest upon him," writes Isaiah, "the spirit of wisdom and understanding, the spirit of counsel and might, the spirit of knowledge and the fear of the Lord" (11:2).[4] Enoch says that "The Lord of Spirits seated him [the Messiah] on the throne of his glory, and the Spirit of righteousness was poured out upon him" (62:2; cf. 49:3). And John the Baptist, who heralded the last days, spoke of one soon to come who would baptize "with the Holy Spirit and with fire" (Matt. 3:11; Luke 3:16).

The Kingdom, then, breaks in with power. God's vicegerent will reign with power. And Jesus' followers read the signs of their times, and the signs of his life and ministry, and knew that the last days had come — *as did Jesus himself!*

His baptism was divine commissioning and divine empowering — and this to make ready (hurry, repent) for the Kingdom's early arrival: "he saw the heavens opened and the Spirit descending upon him like a dove" (Mark 1:10). In his first "sermon," he announced the crisis moment of world history:

> The Spirit of the Lord is upon me, because he has anointed me to . . . proclaim the acceptable year of the Lord (Luke 4:18,19).

And after closing the book, his first words were these: "Today this scripture has been fulfilled in your hearing" (vs. 21). It was the Spirit of the last days which impelled his mission. And he understood his ministry as, in the most immediate sense, a channel of that Spirit, his words and deeds imparting the powerful threat and promise of divine sovereignty: "But if it is by the Spirit (finger) of God that I cast out demons, then the kingdom of God has come upon you" (Matt. 12:28; Luke 11:20). And all this was not just something which Jesus "thought." The power of his words, the effectiveness of his works, the way in which he somehow seemed to penetrate the lives of others — this was something witnessed, a personal reality to those who knew him in Galilee and Judea.[5] After the

[4] See above, p. 40, fn. 8.
[5] See above, pp. 54–9.

Resurrection, there was no longer any doubt. He was the bearer of God's Holy Spirit, the Messiah.

Awareness of the Spirit was a dominant characteristic of primitive Christianity. According to Acts, the Pentecostal gift was the first significant event in the life of the Church as Church. In the same book, every critical juncture of the tiny community's growth and expansion is attributed to the Spirit: the appointing of the seven "deacons," the conversion of Paul, Peter's first preaching to Gentiles, the inception of Paul's first missionary journey, subsequent decisions in his travels, the crucial decree of the council at Jerusalem.[6]

But there is more. Every facet of human experience as now *Christian* experience is the work of the Spirit. Baptism transmits the Spirit: "But it is God who . . . has put his seal upon us and given us his Spirit in our hearts as a guarantee" (II Cor. 1:21,22; cf. Acts 2:38). Church membership is a sharing in the Spirit: "The grace of the Lord Jesus Christ and the love of God and the fellowship of the Holy Spirit be with you all" (II Cor. 13:14; cf. Phil. 2:1). Ecstatic expressions, such as prophesying and speaking with tongues, are "gifts of the Spirit," puzzling to us, but none the less evidence of the intensity of early Christian conviction (I Cor. 12–14; Acts 2:1–13).

But more important, permanent essential qualities of Christian living are equally gifts of the Spirit, such things as "love, joy, peace, patience, kindness, goodness, faithfulness, gentleness, self-control" (Gal. 5:22). So too with Paul's famous triad, faith, hope, and love (I Cor. 13:13). The Christian lives "in Christ" and "in the Spirit" — two Pauline phrases which are virtually identical. He walks "in" or "by the Spirit," is "led by the Spirit" (Gal. 5:16,18,25; Rom. 8:14).

[6] Acts 6:3–6; 9:17; 10:19,44–48; 11:12–18; 13:2–4; 15:28; 16:6–10; 19:21; 20:22,23; etc.

These are all matters to be detailed as we proceed. And they all point to one overwhelming certainty — the Kingdom had actually dawned. The present gift of the Spirit was only a beginning, but it was the real thing — so real that life was a new creation, and hope for the future absolutely sure. Had not Jesus said that man must and could live the life of the Kingdom ("Follow me!") even while waiting for its full coming? It was true.

III

The Church

Always the New Testament assumes that life "in the Spirit" is life in community. The biblical writers do not argue the point. There is, for that matter, every likelihood that Jesus did not envisage or found a new formal ecclesiastical organization. Church, however, is of the very warp and woof of the New Testament witness to God's Messiah. And still today Church remains an essential part of total Christian living. Why?

The answer, in brief, is this. Jesus' own heritage from Judaism, and his own gospel, alike presupposed people in community. Church is an inevitable result of his life and teaching.

Semitic peoples were realistically and intensely aware of the corporate aspect of human life. So important were group solidarity, clan, family, that oftentimes, when no actual relationship existed, one was artificially created by means of solemn contracts sealed with blood. Behind this and, of course, not consciously formulated, was awareness of something of the greatest importance — the fact that no individual can live unto himself, more than this, that to be a full person demands community. The concept of "peoplehood" bespeaks something essential to the human circumstance.

Israel shared in this view. But of special significance is her particular stress upon the fact of community as something willed and given by God. So, of course, she had understood her own history. It was to be a special *people* that Yahweh had called the nation's forebears out of Egypt and made a covenant with them: "Now therefore, if you will obey my voice and keep my covenant, you shall be my own possession among all peoples . . ." (Ex. 19:5). Her own "peoplehood," then, was of God, and a theocracy, because ultimately God was her King — which is to say that Israel was a Church. For Church means a community consciously "under God." And, theoretically, there was no time when Israel was other than God's people. To most Jews of Jesus' day, our concept of the separation of Church and state would have been utterly incomprehensible.

But Church is more than just a theocratic community. It is a community which worships, and seeks to do God's will. God is holy; the covenant obligates Israel to be holy. And the summary of God's demand is this: "Thou shalt love the Lord thy God . . . and thy neighbor as thyself." [1]

The biblical view, then, exalts the fact of human sociality to a triangle: Everyman, his neighbor, *and* God! This is Church, theocracy, community consciously admitting God's sovereignty and obeying. And it is only "in Church," that is, by living the triangle life, that any individual can know salvation, become that full person that God intends.

History shows that Israel was far from being a perfect Church. Often she broke the covenant relationship, apostatized, and knew God's judgment. But always there was hope for the future. In His good time the Kingdom would be all in all. And a kingdom means people, in this case a community truly wel-

[1] See above, pp. 18–20 f.

coming God's sovereignty. Often, then, the prophets spoke of a new Israel, continuous with the old, but different, because no longer gainsaying and disobedient, a remnant with a new covenant, a true theocracy. The idea of Church was an inseparable part of Judaism's future hope.

This, too, was the heritage of Jesus who announced the advent of God's Kingdom. True, he was critical of some of the liturgical details and ethical codifications which were part of the ecclesiasticism of his day.[2] At the same time, he lived within the framework of formal Judaism, worshiped in synagogue and temple, and we may safely presume never dreamed of doing otherwise.

But far more important is the fact that Jesus summarized God's sovereign will with the same affirmation which was the core of theocratic Judaism: "thou shalt love the Lord thy God . . . and thy neighbor as thyself." [3] Even more significant, this, as we have seen, was the shape of his own existence, utter submission to God, even to the cross, in order fully and freely to serve others. His own life, that is, was corporate life under God. What is sometimes called the simple "I-Thou" relationship between an individual and deity is but a half truth. Full "personhood" demands "peoplehood." Such was Jesus' gospel. And it was this, his "triangle-Church" life, through which was mediated the power which others encountered in him. Christian "personhood," then, is "peoplehood" under the God and Father of Jesus Christ. To be "in Christ" is to be a member of the Church.

In this connection, Jesus' last meal on the night of his betrayal has particular significance. For here, indeed, was met the Church — both that of the old covenant, and the new. And if

[2] See above, pp. 20, 97 f.
[3] See above, pp. 18 f.

any one point in history can be underlined as the moment when the new was founded, this was it. Here are important texts:

> Truly, I say to you, I shall not drink again of the fruit of the vine until that day when I drink it new in the kingdom of God (Mark 14:25).

> This is my body which is broken for you. Do this in remembrance of me. . . . This cup is the new covenant in my blood. . . . (I Cor. 11:24,25).

> Behold, the days are coming, says the Lord, when I will make a new covenant with the house of Israel and the house of Judah (Jer. 31:31).

The Last Supper was held in the shadow of the cross. It was the final time when Jesus and the few who were left to him would be together in that same relationship which they had known over the past months. And what he did in that upper room was a dramatic and never to be forgotten reaffirmation of what his whole life had been.

He must die; it was God's inscrutable will that, for the Kingdom, he must sacrifice everything. But "I [*shall*] drink it new in the kingdom of God!" So Jesus underlined again his own faith in God as King. And he accepted his death ("I shall not drink again"), for, at any cost, God's sovereignty is the one thing that matters. "Thou shalt love the Lord thy God."

But his death, again as his entire life, was a reaffirmation of the King's other demand, too. "This is my body — it is I myself — broken *for you*." The Kingdom, when it comes, will be for the blessing of many. To welcome God's reign is always a thing of joy. Jesus' ministry had sought to prepare people to accept that joy. Somehow, in God's providence his death would effect this, too. "Thou shalt love thy neighbor" — he died, as he lived, as Servant of all.

Calvary, then, was not an event that stands out in splendid and tragic isolation, but rather the climactic doing of what

Jesus had been doing all along, and the climactic fulfillment of what, all along, he had been. The cross was his final proclamation — that God is King, and that full "personhood," true life, risen life, salvation, means life in community consciously welcoming God's kingship, and obeying.

All this, however, was more than a final proclamation. It was a solemn compact which pointed beyond Calvary. "This cup is the *new* covenant in my blood" — the one that had been long awaited and long promised for the time when the Kingdom, centering upon a true people of God, should come (Jer. 31:31). Here was not an end, but a beginning — and the disciples, who shared the bread and the cup with him, knew it.

Often, during the earthly ministry, Jesus and his followers had eaten together and, as we know from our own experience, this kind of sharing in a very special way binds people together. Already, then, before that last night, the bonds had been forged. To be with him for those brief months, despite the incompleteness of their understanding, had been to discern something of what it means to accept God's kingship, to sense, also, something of the joy and the pain and the power of dying to one's self in order to serve God and neighbor. And now, in the upper room, and shadowed by the cross, few words were needed. His promise that he would drink again in the Kingdom, the sharing of the bread and the cup with them now as, so often, they had shared everything in the past, and all this against the backdrop of all that he had taught and been — they understood, even though, for the moment, perhaps dimly. That sharing with him and with one another was to continue. And the *new* covenant which this last moment together represented, and which the cross and the Resurrection sealed, was this — God's confirmation that what Jesus had said was true, that what he had done was from above, that what he had come to mean in their lives was incontrovertible reality, that love is all-powerful to forgive and to restore, and that in love for God and man is wondrous undreamed-of life.

It was this, God's own love for His world, God's way for His world, which was covenanted that night — the triangle life, the Christ life, the Church life, the Church herself.

It comes as no surprise, then, that Jesus' followers understood the Last Supper as a command to "do this in remembrance of me." The Greek word employed here is *anamnēsis,* and means far more than "in memory of" or "as a memorial to."· In Semitic usage, "the recollection of the past means that what is recalled becomes a present reality," and "cult is sacred memory becoming sacred reality and life for the participants." [4] The fact that early Christians used this word *anamnēsis,* then, can mean but one thing — that it was in the breaking of bread that the crucified-risen one, and all that he had been and continued to be, was most real to them. And it is no wonder that the Church has always been most truly and fully herself when she breaks that bread and blesses that cup.[5]

Did Jesus found the Church? This is a question which would have startled the first believers. No word of command was necessary. Church was an inseparable part of the life which he lived, of the gospel which he proclaimed, and of those lives which witnessed his earthly ministry. Church and salvation are one.

IV

Baptism for the Forgiveness of
Sins — Salvation as Past Event

To receive the Spirit, to become a member of the new people of God, was to have one's feet set on a fresh path. And spe-

[4] G. Henton Davies, "Memorial, Memory," in *The Interpreter's Dictionary of the Bible,* Abingdon Press, Nashville, Tenn., 1962. Vol. 3, pp. 344 f.
[5] See below, pp. 196 f.

cifically, it was one's baptism which brought this about. The Nicene Creed is explicit: "I acknowledge one Baptism for the remission of sins." Behind the less specific "forgiveness of sins" in the shorter formulary lies the same conviction — baptism is the moment when the believer is saved. It is the story of baptism which we must trace in the next few pages.

Jesus was not the first in his day to cry "repent." His forerunner, John, also proclaimed the imminence of the Kingdom, stressing particularly the element of divine judgment: "Even now the ax is laid to the root of the trees; every tree therefore that does not bear good fruit is cut down and thrown into the fire" (Matt. 3:10; Luke 3:9). At the same time, John offered hope. If his hearers would turn from their past and undergo purification in the form of "baptism of repentance for the forgiveness of sins," they need not fear. Many heeded this call, and "were baptized by him in the river Jordan, confessing their sins" (Mark 1:4,5).

Jesus of Nazareth came, heard John's message, answered his call, and was baptized (Mark 1:9-11; Matt. 3:13-17; Luke 3:21,22). In doing so he accepted John's gospel as pertinent and meaningful for himself, identified himself with those others who recognized the imperative of God's sovereignty, the needs and lacks of their human circumstance, and the fact that all men stand under judgment. Moreover, he knew himself impelled by God's Spirit to proclaim this same call to repentance and obedience.

Contrary to the practice of John, Jesus and his disciples seem not to have baptized others.[1] After the Resurrection, however,

[1] According to John 3:22, "Jesus and his disciples went into the land of Judea; there he remained with them and baptized." John 4:1,2 reads, "Now when the Lord knew that the Pharisees had heard that Jesus was making and baptizing more disciples than John (although Jesus himself did not baptize, but only his disciples) . . ." Confusion seems to reign. There is no hint elsewhere in the New Testament that Jesus baptized, or that his followers did so during the earthly ministry. The brevity of that ministry, and the urgent haste with which it was carried out, as well as the confusion in the Johannine tradition, all suggest that Christian baptism did not enter into the picture until after the Resurrection. We have already noted that Matt. 28:19 could hardly have been uttered by Jesus himself (pp. 16 f.).

water baptism soon became a prerequisite for entrance into the Church. Saul of Tarsus was baptized within three or four days of his conversion on the Damascus Road (Acts 9:18). The pattern which we have noted in the sermons of Acts (repent and be baptized) reflects very early practice.[2] Several circumstances combined to bring this about.

In the first place, it was a natural pattern for Christians of Jewish background to follow. In Jesus' day, Gentiles were generally required to undergo not only circumcision, but also a water lustration rite which both effected that ritual purification required by Jewish law and served as an act of repentance and consecration to the moral standards of Israel.

Closer to home, however, is the water baptism of John. Actually, we know little about this rite. It differed, of course, from proselyte baptism, because it was primarily for those already Jews, and had a quite different purpose, preparation for the immediate advent of God's Kingdom (Matt. 3:7-10; Luke 3:7-9). Even after his death it continued to be administered by the "Baptist Sect," followers of John who continued his work.[3] And there is little doubt that early Christian practice owes something to John's water baptism. One would expect this, for both groups had the same concern — repentance as preparation for the Kingdom and its Messiah. Moreover, at least one of Jesus' closest followers, Andrew, had been a disciple of the Baptist until the Galilean appeared on the scene (John 1:35-40).

It was, however, the fact that Jesus had himself been baptized which constituted the chief ground root for the Christian practice. Here, rather than in any formal command (which Jesus almost certainly did not give), lies the sure "dominical authority" for the Church's sacrament.

Underlining this fact are suggestive parallels between Jesus' own understanding of his baptism and the significance which early Christian converts saw in their own. He, for example,

[2] See above, pp. 158 f.
[3] See Acts 18:25 and 19:3,4. A careful scrutiny of the relations between Jesus and John as recorded in the Gospel tradition shows that the latter was a far more prominent figure than is generally recognized.

identified himself with those to whose need John spoke and "in this *corporate* sense," as one writer puts it, "we may say that even for him baptism expressed repentance." [4] And the primitive Church understood her rite as a radical turning from the present, "the forgiveness of sins" (Acts 2:38, etc.). It was at this moment that Jesus' awareness of filial relationship crystallized as a call to special vocation. And again, early Christians believed themselves to be adopted as sons of God at baptism.[5] For Jesus it was a moment, too, of special consecration and empowering for his task. So, as well, for the Christian convert — at baptism he received the Spirit.

How, specifically, did the first believers understand this rite? It was, for one thing, a visible profession of repentance and of moral reorientation in response to the good news that the Kingdom was at hand. Both John and Jesus had cried "repent." Both had sought to make ready a special people who would welcome the great event.

But with this any similarity between the two rites comes to an end. For Christian baptism was one of water *and* the Spirit. It has even been plausibly suggested that at the very beginning believers spoke of the charismatic experience of the Spirit as a "baptism" which was superior to John's water rite, something which proved that Jesus was the greater of the two prophetic figures. Initially, that is, water baptism and Spirit baptism may have been two different things (Johannine versus Christian) which soon, for the reasons suggested above, merged to form the Christian rite of water and the Spirit.

Be this as it may, it was not long before the traditional pattern emerged. We can see it in the already mentioned Petrine

[4] W. F. Flemington, *The New Testament Doctrine of Baptism*, London, S.P.C.K., 1957, p. 121.
[5] See above, pp. 76 f.

exhortations.[6] Paul assumes it as long-established practice.[7] In the Fourth Gospel the pattern appears as the word of Jesus himself: "Truly, truly . . . unless one is born of water and the Spirit, he cannot enter the kingdom of God" (3:5). Through baptism, then, the convert is made a member of that people which even now knows the joy and the power of the age to come.

Another important accent of the primitive rite is expressed by the frequent reference to baptism "in the name of Jesus." In addition to the frequently cited Acts 2:38, this practice is implied by Acts 4:12, a passage, incidentally, which shows the rite to be an absolute prerequisite for Church membership: "And there is salvation in no one else, for there is no other name under heaven given among men by which we must be saved." That the Apostle Paul knows this custom is evident from his questions, "Is Christ divided? Was Paul crucified for you? Or were you baptized in the name of Paul?" (I Cor. 1:13).

The reference is to an actual pronouncing of the name of the candidate's new Lord (in precisely what form is difficult to say) over the convert at the moment of his immersion. Note the words of James 2:7 which probably should be rendered, "Do they not blaspheme the honorable name which has been spoken over you?" Nor was this "naming" a mere formality. Christian practice here was strongly influenced by the Hebraic view that a person's name was not just an identifying label, but a kind of semi-personification of the bearer which mediated something of the reality which lay behind it.

Baptism, then, signified the beginning of a personal relationship between the convert and the risen Lord. The candidate was sealed, stamped with the name, designated as the "property" of Christ, placed under his protection. More than this, the

[6] See above, pp. 158 f.
[7] See, for example, Rom. 6:3,4; 8:15; I Cor. 10:1,2; 12:13; II Cor. 1:21,22; Gal. 4:6.

name mediated the power of its owner. In part, perhaps, this custom owes its origin to Christian experience that baptism was an empowering with the Spirit.[8]

Over and beyond this, the "naming" stands as the primitive Church's first movement towards a theological and sacramental interpretation of baptism as the moment when the candidate received forgiveness for the past. The "name," that is, was viewed as a power which removed sin.

Important here is the practice, widespread in the Mediterranean world at that time, of exorcism by the use of magical formulae and occult acts. We recall, too, that many of Jesus' mighty works took the form of exorcisms which cast out evil spirits who caused sin and its effects. Of particular significance for us at the moment is the fact that Jesus' own name was sometimes employed as the key word in exorcistic formulae.

Luke, for example, records this incident: "Master, we saw a man casting out demons *in your name,* and we forbade him, because he does not follow with us" (9:49; cf. Mark 9:38 ff.). Peter heals a cripple "in the *name* of Jesus Christ of Nazareth," and goes on to explain that "his *name,* by faith in his *name,* has made this man strong" (Acts 3:6,16). Generally, signs and wonders were attributed to "the *name* of [God's] holy servant Jesus" (Acts 4:30). And once we have the assertion that remission of sins comes "through his *name*" (Acts 10:43).[9]

The ministry of Jesus was one of healing forgiveness. Christian baptism was "for the forgiveness of sins," and "in the *name* of Jesus." The significance of this conjunction of ideas needs no detailing. Still today in Roman Catholic practice, exorcism

[8] See especially II Cor. 1:22: "he [God] has put his seal upon us and given us his Spirit in our hearts as a guarantee." The reference is to baptism. In baptismal rites today, the candidate is signed (sealed) with the sign of the cross on his forehead in the name of the Trinity. There is a close connection between being baptized "in the name," and "into Christ" (Rom. 6:3, etc.), and Paul's concept of life "in Christ" as "life in the Spirit" (see below pp. 181–6). For to be "in Christ" is to belong to him and to be dominated by the Spirit.

[9] See further, Mark 6:7, 16:17, Acts 16:18, 19:13. Italics mine.

174

is a part of the baptismal rite. And all this is an important part of the pre-history of our current practice of baptizing in the *name* of the Trinity, a formula which Matthew's Gospel shows had begun to emerge before the close of the first century (28:19).

We have been detailing an early tradition of baptismal sin-remission. But, as we noted earlier, there was another primitive "sin theology," one centering upon the cross: "Christ died for our sins." [10] These two traditions were, at first, quite unrelated. Before long, however, they were merged, and the juncture represents a highly significant development of New Testament baptismal theology. What happened, in brief, was this. Christians explained baptism of repentance in the name of Jesus as the moment when each candidate received the benefit of Jesus' atoning death: "Christ died for *me*!" The result was sharply to underline the importance of the rite itself, and to delineate its theological significance much more precisely and richly.

The believer, then, looked back to the moment of baptism as a decisive one. It was at that time that he had made explicit his response of faith to the Church's proclamation of God and Christ (Articles 1 and 2), had been forgiven for all that was past, received newness of life as a member of the community of the Spirit. He had been saved.

This deeper understanding of baptism is especially clear in the following texts: [11]

> Do you not know that all of us who have been baptized into Christ Jesus were baptized into his death? We were buried therefore with him by baptism into death, so that as Christ was raised from the dead by the glory of the Father, we too might walk in newness of life (Rom. 6:3,4).

[10] See above, pp. 118–31.
[11] See also Gal. 3:27; Eph. 2:5,6; II Tim. 2:11; I Pt. 3:21.

> In him also you were circumcised with a circumcision made
> without hands, by putting off the body of flesh in the cir-
> cumcision of Christ; and you were buried with him in
> baptism, in which you were also raised with him through
> faith in the working of God, who raised him from the
> dead (Col. 2:11,12).

The picture here is a vivid one. The candidate's complete immersion (the normal practice in those days) is likened to a
burial, as Jesus was buried on Good Friday. And as his was a
death "for our sins," so for the convert, baptism is his personal
expression of need and of faith, and thus his own death to self
and sin "in Christ." Baptism, then, is the moment when the
powerful forgiveness of the Christ life is mediated to those who
call upon his name (Rom. 10:9–13).

But "in Christ" means the Resurrection, too. So the candidate
emerges from the water to a new risen life. Jesus "was put to
death for our trespasses and raised for our justification" (Rom.
4:25). The past, then, is forgiven; at last the convert's feet are
set on the path of a new righteousness. He knows salvation.

The passage from Colossians uses the same imagery. But in
addition, baptism is described as analogous to circumcision.
The Jew looked upon the latter as a special mark of identity,
a sealing that set him off as one of God's chosen people destined
to share in all the special benefits of the covenant and the
promises. But now there is a new external rite, a different kind
of sealing, and appropriately so, because there is a new Israel,
the Christian Church. So, as Paul says elsewhere in dialogue
with those who argued that all converts should, as a part of
their new faith, accept circumcision and the Jewish law, the old
external rite has been superseded.[12] At the same time, as a "circumcision made without hands," baptism is the moment of
initiation into the new chosen race, the sealing and ratification
of the new covenant in Christ's blood, and so an utterly new
beginning.

[12] See above, pp. 127 f.

This concept of baptism as a dying and rising with Christ represents one of the contributions of the wider Mediterranean world view to Christian thought. Whether or not Paul is responsible for this particular imagery is uncertain. But as one who grew up in cosmopolitan Tarsus outside Palestine, his ready acceptance of this baptismal idiom reminds us of the Church's rapid expansion and fruitful dialogue with the Hellenistic thought world. In the various mystery cults, for example, through sacramental rites initiates were believed to share in the fate of a deity who had suffered death and then returned to life. So the devotees were enabled to attain that for which they longed, a blissful immortality, salvation. Similarity with the Christian interpretation of baptism is self-evident.

At the same time, the Christian mystery — we need have no reluctance to use this term — is a very different thing. For it has its origin not in legend, but in real history, in things which actually happened. Myth and poetry, of course, have played a role. There was (and is) no other way of expressing depths of meaning which defy the neat packaging of our earth-bound minds. But there actually was a Jesus of Nazareth! Moreover, he can still be seen and known — the earthly Jesus — through the Church's tradition, and Christian theology insists that to know him as such (truly man) is absolutely fundamental.

To see the connection, then, between Paul's understanding of baptism, and the life and teaching of Jesus himself is important. And we can see it, and clearly, too, for all that the Church's later language differs from that of the earthly ministry. These texts are important:

> If any man would come after me, let him deny himself and take up his cross and follow me. For whoever would save his life will lose it; and whoever loses his life for my sake and the gospel's will save it (Mark 8:34,35).

> The cup that I drink you will drink; and with the baptism [a reference to being immersed in suffering and tribula-

tion] with which I am baptized, you will be baptized (Mark 10:39).

Let God reign; to do so is salvation — this was Jesus' teaching. This, too, with its inevitable corollary of death to the wrong kind of self and oftentimes painful concern for others, was his life, the Death-Resurrection Christ life. Such became the life of every convert when he died and rose with Christ in the baptismal waters.

Closely related to the Death-Resurrection imagery is another, baptism understood as new birth, regeneration. This particular idiom came into prominence toward the end of the New Testament period. Most of the texts, as those below, appear in books written long after Paul's missionary career came to an end:

> Truly, truly, I say to you, unless one is born anew (from above) . . . of water and the Spirit, he cannot enter the kingdom of God (John 3:3-5; cf. John 1:12,13).

> But when the goodness and loving kindness of God our Savior appeared, he saved us, not because of deeds done by us in righteousness, but in virtue of his own mercy, by the washing of regeneration and renewal in the Holy Spirit, which he poured out upon us richly through Jesus Christ our Savior (Tit. 3:4-6; cf. I Pt. 1:3,23).

This idiom, like the concept of dying and rising, underlines the manner in which believers looked upon salvation as an accomplished fact, and baptism as the moment when it had occurred. It depicts, too, the utter newness of the Christian life in faith — for there is nothing on the purely physical plane more decisive than birth and death. Already one had entered the Kingdom. Life now, even though still in this world, was "from above." To confess Jesus as God's Messiah made things inexpressibly different.

178

Here again the Christian imagery owes not a little to antecedents. In Judaism the conversion of a Gentile was sometimes termed a rebirth, proselytes being spoken of as "new-born children." Regeneration also was a part of the common parlance of the Hellenistic religions, for example, in the mysteries of Isis and Attis.

But again, the starting point for all this is the teaching of Jesus. Note this text:

> Truly . . . whoever does not receive the kingdom of God
> like a child shall not enter it (Mark 10:15).

It is not spotless innocence, or naïveté, of which these words speak. Rather, the absolute prerequisite for salvation is that kind of total trust and total commitment which is characteristic of the very young. Faith in God must be the bedrock of one's life. This is death to self, to be born anew. And to become regenerate in baptism is to know one's past to be truly past, and to enter into a life as different from that which was before as is day from night. Such is the re-creative power of that forgiveness which the believer encounters in Jesus Christ.

To express deepest intangible reality in concrete form is one of the necessities of the human circumstance. Only in this way can one make that reality intelligible to himself, or communicate it to others. Soon, then, the rite of baptism became a focal point of the salvation experience. It was then that the convert confessed his faith in God and Christ (Articles 1, 2), and commenced his new life in the community of the Spirit (Article 3). This was the moment of moments. He had been saved.

V

The Church as Holy, Catholic, Communion
of Saints — Salvation Through Striving

The Kingdom had dawned, a new people had been created, the Spirit had been received, salvation had come. And yet, any convert who imagined that baptism would impart immunity against either temptation or any of the other hard realities of life must soon have become sadly disillusioned. Repeatedly the biblical writers refer to the sins of believers, rebuke, exhort, even threaten.

At Corinth, there were Christians who hauled each other before the law courts, drank too much wine when they assembled for the community meals at which the primitive Eucharist was celebrated, went all-out to undermine Paul's authority. In Thessalonica, there were busybodies who lived on the doles of other members of the community. Ananias and Sapphira were cheats. The rich humiliated the poor and played favorites.[1] It was all very well to talk about being saved, of dying once and for all to sin. But facts were facts, and people were people — even Christians. For this, too, we have only to look at the New Testament.

Clearly, salvation, no matter what one might think or wish, was not a once-for-all gift mechanically received and automatically operative.[2] That which had been initiated at baptism was not a kind of immunity, but a new beginning with power,

[1] See, for example, I Cor. 6:1–8, 11:17–22,33,34, 1:10–17, 3:10–15, II Th. 3:6–15, Acts 5:1–11, Jas. 2:1–13.

[2] See Paul's warning with respect to baptism in I Cor. 10:1–13. His words about circumcision (Rom. 2:25–29) are equally relevant for the Christian as warning against any idea of automatic salvation through the use of rites and ceremonies.

dying and rising with Christ not something done once and for all, but decisive entry into a new pattern of daily living. Still one had to struggle, and almost every page of the New Testament reflects this, too. Salvation was not a means of escaping the world, but a way of facing up to it.[3]

As so often, Paul is our best exemplar. He obviously knows first-hand the problem posed by the paradoxical "now — not yet" of the new life: the Kingdom had dawned, but was still fully to be realized. And in particular, his own experience of salvation as struggle forged two concepts which have been rich treasures ever since: Christianity as life "in the Spirit — in Christ," and the Church as "one Body of Christ." More than anything else, these insights sum up the fact that salvation is a wondrous "becoming-of-what-one-already-is" which must be proved by fire.

It is almost impossible for us to comprehend the intensity of earliest Christian faith and the vividness of the Parousia hope. Salvation had come — really! At any moment Jesus would return on the clouds in full glory. But he didn't! It couldn't be that they were wrong — and yet, were they?

We must remember that most of the early believers, for all their sincerity, were relatively unlettered. Moreover, there had been neither time nor need (surely Jesus would re-appear tomorrow!) for thinking out the deep implications of what had happened. It is no wonder that there began to develop signs of frustration and disappointment — and doubts.

Here is where Paul enters the picture. One might expect that he would meet the tension of the "now — not yet" by soft-pedaling the former and underlining the latter. But he does just the opposite. He takes the "now" of Christian experience,

[3] This recalls the Hebraic concept of all history as a means of encounter with God. See above, pp. 32–43.

strips it of its encumbrances, and focuses upon it such a bright light, that neither delay nor adverse circumstances could ever again obscure it. God had in truth visited and redeemed His people. Christ had in fact made all the difference in the world. The love of God had irresistibly and permanently penetrated their hearts through the Holy Spirit. Here were facts which nothing could change.

What did it mean, actually, to have received the Spirit of the new age? Was it just a promise of things to come? Was its purpose simply to make life happy, to produce a kind of intoxicated ecstasy? It does do these things; nor are such ecstatic manifestations as prophecy and speaking with tongues to be despised: "I thank God that I speak in tongues more than you all" (I Cor. 14:18). But there are more important gifts of the Spirit — faith and hope, and above all love. In short, Paul "ethicizes" the Spirit.

This is clear from his repeated stress upon Christian life as "in," "by," "according to" the Spirit. Here are a few samples:

For by one Spirit we were all baptized into one body — Jews or Greeks, slaves or free — and all were made to drink of one Spirit (I Cor. 12:13; cf. Rom. 8:15; Gal. 4:6; II Cor. 1:22).

But you are not in the flesh, you are in the Spirit, if the Spirit of God really dwells in you. Any one who does not have the Spirit of Christ does not belong to him (Rom. 8:9).

Do you not know that you are God's temple and that God's Spirit dwells in you (I Cor. 3:16)?

But I say, walk by the Spirit, and do not gratify the desires of the flesh. . . . If we live by the Spirit, let us also walk by the Spirit (Gal. 5:16–25; cf. Rom. 12:11; 14:17).

For those who live according to the flesh set their minds on the things of the flesh, but those who live according to the Spirit set their minds on the things of the Spirit (Rom. 8:5).

What is Paul saying here? This — the Spirit received at baptism is both permanent possession and continually operative in the believer's life. Most had thought of it as something that made itself felt only occasionally, almost erratically, at special moments or for special purposes — healing, prophecy, and such like. But, the Apostle says, this is the least important thing. The Spirit is *dunamis* — permanent power for moment by moment Christian living.

When Paul speaks of life "by," "in," "according to the Spirit," he is saying far more than comes through in the literal translation. The original Greek prepositions point to their object as the chief fact of one's existence. To be "in the Spirit" does not mean immersion in a fog of piety or good feeling, but to have one's self dominated and impelled by a divine dynamic. And here the importance of Paul's "ethicizing" becomes clear. The chief spiritual gifts are not those which manifest themselves as temporary ecstasies, but such enduring constancies as faith, hope, love: "But the fruit of the Spirit is love, joy, peace, patience, kindness, goodness, faithfulness, gentleness, self-control" (I Cor. 13:13; Gal. 5:22, 23). The Kingdom of God is *here-and-now* "righteousness and peace and joy in the Holy Spirit" (Rom. 14:17).

This Pauline stress upon the power of the Spirit as continuously present in the Christian life is especially important. It serves as a basis for some of the deepest insights which we find in Holy Scripture, passages which show how profound were Paul's own commitment and experience as one of the religious greats of all time.

For one thing, Paul's "ethicizing" of the Spirit enabled him to face up to the problem of sin both realistically and optimistically. He knew perfectly well that as long as one is in this world, the pull to be dominated by the world (to live "according to the flesh") will be very real: "For the desires of the flesh are against the Spirit, and the desires of the Spirit are against the flesh; for these are opposed to each other, to prevent you from doing what you would" (Gal. 5:17; cf. Rom. 7:13–25). The word "desires" in the original Greek (the verb *epithumein*) expresses extreme intensity. The temptation to be dominated by the world has a fierceness to it which Paul himself knew full well.

But the Christian now has hope; for his changed life is dominated by a new power unto righteousness, his true being "from above." One can still yield to temptation — and let no one forget, there is judgment; but he can overcome. The Christian life is not automatic sinlessness — but a new and unshakable confidence and power and hope.

But life "in the Spirit" involves something else — the fact that salvation cannot become a reality without genuine concern for others. The chief gift of the Spirit is outgoing love (I Cor. 13:13). And this gift must be used, for the only thing that "avails" for the Christian is "faith energizing through love" (Gal. 5:6).[4] Here, in other words, is the triangle life: the divine Spirit — Everyman — neighbor. It is God's way that full "personhood" (salvation) demands "peoplehood."[5]

As a consequence, "works" *are* supremely important for the believer. It is true that "justification is by faith." Man can never earn or deserve that which God gives; and divine forgiveness, too, is a free gift. But the argument which some threw in Paul's face — that since God freely forgives if and whenever one asks it, then it matters little what a man does with his daily life — is completely to misunderstand his intent with respect to justification and atonement.[6] Divine forgiveness is an action of personal love. And the acceptance of that love (which is one way of saying what faith is!) carries with it a burning desire to do the will of Him who forgives and loves. Thus he who receives knows the doing of works to be a divine imperative. James wrote, "So faith by itself, if it has no works, is dead" —

[4] See also John 15:12 f.; I John 4:20.
[5] See above, pp. 164–9.
[6] See, for example, Rom. 3:1–8, 6:1 f., 15 f. See above, pp. 126–31; see also below, pp. 214 f.

and with this Paul would have agreed wholeheartedly (2:17).

The Apostle's concept of the Spirit, then, underlined both the power and the importance of the believer's "now." No matter how long the Parousia was delayed, every present instant offered a meaningful task, was a moment of vocation. And yet there was something lacking. For all its richness, life "in the Spirit" is a concept abstract and impersonal — and Paul sensed this. Thus, out of his own deeply personal religious experience there emerged his understanding of life "in Christ." These passages are especially illuminating:

> For as many of you as were baptized into Christ have put On Christ (Gal. 3:27; cf. Rom. 6:3,4).
>
> so we, though many, are one body in Christ . . . (Rom. 12:5).
>
> I have been crucified with Christ; it is no longer I who live, but Christ who lives in me . . . (Gal. 2:20).
>
> But you are not in the flesh, you are in the Spirit, if the Spirit of God really dwells in you. And one who does not have the Spirit of Christ does not belong to him (Rom. 8:9; cf. II Cor. 3:17).
>
> For you have died, and your life is hid with Christ in God (Col. 3:3).

These texts are strikingly similar to those above on page 182. Instead of being baptized into the Spirit, one is baptized into Christ. The believer lives "in Christ," and Christ lives in the believer, as also does the Spirit. The Christian belongs to Christ.[7] In other words, to be "in the Spirit" and "in Christ" are virtually one and the same thing, and Paul, as is especially apparent in Romans 8:9, moves easily from one concept to the other. And what Paul has done here is to "personalize" the Spirit. We must look at this further.

In his letters, he uses the phrase "in Christ," including such

[7] This recalls baptism "in the name of Jesus." See above, pp. 173 f.

parallel expressions as "in the Lord" and "in him," some one hundred fifty times.[8] Here is the center of his own experience, his apprehension that Christianity is ultimately a relation of *persons* — that God is *personal,* and that it is through knowing a particular *person,* Jesus Christ, that there is saving knowledge of God. "Christ in you, the hope of glory"; "we have the mind of Christ"; "you . . . have put on Christ"; "your life is hid with Christ in God" — mystical union is the descriptive phrase often used, and appropriately so (Col. 1:27; I Cor. 2:16; Gal. 3:27; cf. 26–29; Col. 3:3). The writer of the Fourth Gospel uses a different idiom: "I am the vine, you are the branches" (15:5). Between the Christian and his Lord there exists the closest possible relationship, one so rich that for no two individuals does it ever mean quite the same thing.

Recalling, now, that "in Christ" and "in the Spirit" are two different ways of describing essentially the same thing, Paul's "personalizing" of the Spirit, as we termed it above, can be seen in all its depths. That which demands, inspires, commands obedience and allegiance, is not an abstract power, but the dynamic love of a person, the risen Christ — one who can be intimately known and loved, because he is the same loved one who lived and died and was "eyewitnessed" in Palestine. Note how Paul all but equates love (something which can be only between persons) with the Spirit: "God's love has been poured into our hearts through the Holy Spirit which has been given to us" (Rom. 5:5). And this is none other than the love of Jesus himself who, Paul says, "loved me and gave himself for me" (Gal. 2:20). To be "in Christ" was to find that Jesus' call, "Follow me," had inexpressible meaningfulness.

But again, to be "in Christ" means to be "in the Spirit," which means to know a divine imperative and empowering for ethical behavior. According to Paul, the Christian knows and receives Christ's love, which is God's love, and returns it as person to person. But also, love is outgoing, and love is the chief gift of

[8] See above, pp. 63 f.

the Spirit.[9] This says something very important about what it means to be "in Christ." Christian mysticism is not static, but dynamic. It turns one's face toward the world, compels one to be up and doing.

This, of course, occasions no surprise. Jesus' life as Servant of others had been the triangle life.[10] From the beginning, to know Christ had been to know one's self forgiven, and a new creation; for he had been (and continued to be) the "incarnation" of love as a power that forgives and re-creates. But this was not something that could be selfishly enjoyed for its own sake. To know Christ was to live the Christ life which accepts God's loving sovereignty and does His will, which is to love others. To know the love of Christ, then, was to be impelled to mediate that same love to others. This was God's way to the risen life of full "personhood." And so salvation involved struggle, was something that could come only as through fire — for to die to self for others was no more easy for the Christian than it was for his Lord, who cried, "Father . . . remove this cup from me" (Mark 14:36).

To be "in the Spirit" is to be in the Christian community. To be "in Christ" is to die and rise anew to a saving relationship with others. This is Church; and, Paul says, the Church is the Body of Christ. The manner in which the following texts assume, imply, interweave each other, is striking:

1. For by one Spirit we were all baptized into one body . . . and all were made to drink of one Spirit (I Cor. 12:13).

2. For as many of you as were baptized into Christ have put on Christ (Gal. 3:27).

[9] See above, p. 184.
[10] See above, pp. 166–9.

187

3. . . . we, though many, are one body in Christ, and in-
dividually members one of another (Rom. 12:5; cf. I
Cor. 12:27).

4. For just as the body is one and has many members, and
all the members of the body, though many, are one body,
so it is with Christ (I Cor. 12:12).

In baptism one receives the Spirit and becomes a member of
the Church (No. 1). This also is to clothe oneself with Christ
(No. 2). Since, however, Christ is one, and each member is "in
Christ," all the members as Church are one body (Nos. 3, 4).
It follows, finally, that this oneness which is Christ's body is an
inseparable unity of the members one with another, mutually
dependent upon each other, as are the links and parts of the
human body (Nos. 3, 4).

Close to the surface here, and something of which Paul was
doubtless aware, is a Stoic analogy — a commonwealth, sometimes the whole world, depicted as a human body in which
each single part complements every other part, diversity necessary to and serving a single whole.

More important, however, is the manner in which Paul's
metaphor deepens and "Christianizes" that Semitic mode of
thought which lies at the root of the concept of Church — the
recognition that no man can live unto himself and be a full
person.[11] The concept of the body, then, underlines the Church
as something essential to human experience. It is the New
Testament's most graphic representation of what life as Church
is: God — Everyman — his Neighbor.

Specifically, Paul's idiom stresses the closeness of one's relationship with his Lord, for it is an organic unity which exists
between the parts of the physical body. At the same time, in
Colossians and Ephesians Christ's dominance over the Body is
stressed. He is "the Head, from whom the whole body, nour-
ished and knit together through its joints and ligaments, grows

[11] See above, pp. 164–9.

with a growth that is from God" (Col. 2:19; cf. Eph. 1:22; 5:23–33). Not only is Christ the life and the strength of the Church and of the individual believer, but also that which directs, controls.

Paul also lays particular emphasis upon the relationship of the individual who is "in Christ" with others. He puts it sharply:

> The eye cannot say to the hand, "I have no need of you,"
> nor again the head to the feet, "I have no need of you." . . .
> If one member suffers, all suffer together; if one member
> is honored, all rejoice together (I Cor. 12:21–26).

What one member does is of deep concern to others. The sin of one, the joy of another, affects the whole, and each individual needs all the others. In the Body of Christ believers are "members one of another" (Rom. 12:5).[12]

Again, then, we see that mystical union with Christ is strenuously extrovert and ethical; it does not mean apotheosis, or escape from the world, but rather a being compelled to turn one's face toward the world with new understanding and courage. We have the same stress in the later tradition recorded by John. Salvation comes through union with the true vine; but in the same breath we are told that "Every branch of mine [Christ's] that bears no fruit, he [God] takes away" (John 15:1 ff.). And a few verses further on appear these words: "This is my commandment, that you love one another as I have loved you" (vs. 12). Without Christ, true selfhood is impossible; but it is equally impossible without love for one's neighbor. John and Paul, each in his own way, underline with special effectiveness both the teaching of Jesus and the pattern of his life — that man must love God in relationship with his neighbor.

Both, incidentally, are speaking specifically of the Christian Church, and the relationship of its members to each other. But

[12] See further the discussion of the Church as "The Communion of Saints," pp. 195–7.

the broader implication is clear. Not just one's fellow church-men, but everyone is a neighbor, the object of God's love, and so of the Christian's love. This, too, is true — the Church as a whole cannot live a selfish "I-Thou" relationship with Christ, but has a mission to the remainder of the world. Both Paul and John would have approved of this triangle: God — Church — World! [13]

Two other things, which Paul's metaphor of the Body stresses, are important. First of all is the fact that each member is distinct from the others, and necessarily so: "If the whole body were an eye, where would be the hearing? If the whole body were an ear, where would be the sense of smell?" (I Cor. 12:17). In this same passage Paul speaks of the fact that there are diverse gifts of the Spirit, and not all have the same gifts (vss. 4-11). There is unity (one body) in that these are all manifestations of the one Spirit. Christians are one because they have a common Head, and a common life "in Christ." But each has his own talents, his own irreplaceable contribution to make, his own unique God-given purpose.

One recalls here Jesus' stress upon God's immediate concern for each individual as a person, precious, the only one of his kind: "But even the hairs of your head are all numbered" (Matt. 10:30; cf. 6:24-34). And always the pattern of death to self is not that one may lose all personal identity, but that he may become that wondrous kind of self God means him to be: "whoever loses his life for my sake and the gospel's will save it" (Mark 8:35). So in the Body of Christ, each has his own unique task, a vocation which is fulfilled through his concern for others. So each, in relationship with others, comes to full "personhood."

At the same time, there is in the Church a wiping out of those superficial identification tags which divide and destroy community. Note the following:

There is neither Jew nor Greek, there is neither slave nor
[13] See above, pp. 164-9, and below, pp. 194 f.

free, there is neither male nor female; for you are all one
in Christ Jesus (Gal. 3:28).

For in Christ Jesus neither circumcision nor uncircumcision
is of any avail, but faith working through love (Gal. 5:6).

Words such as these speak for themselves. In true community
under God those accouterments of the human circumstance
which man's sin uses to divide — pride of race or person or
accomplishment or status — are all erased. Nothing matters or
is of ultimate profit or value — neither one's past, nor the par-
ticulars of one's present — except "faith dynamically at work
and proving itself through love" (Gal. 5:6).

To be "in Christ," then, is to be a member of his Body. This
metaphor has told us much, both about the Church herself, and
about that striving unto salvation which is inseparably linked
with community.

In both the Apostles' and Nicene Creeds, the Body of Christ
is termed "Catholic." This precise adjective does not appear in
the New Testament. Its essential content, however, is an integral part of the Apostolic Witness.

"Universal" is the word's root meaning. And inasmuch as
there is one Christ, and one Body of Christ, to proclaim
Catholicity is to affirm that there is but one Church for the entire world. So far as formal organization is concerned, such a
Church does not exist, nor is it likely that it ever will. For that
matter, if one's ecumenical ideal be a monolith of unanimity,
it would be a tragedy if it ever were realized. For the tension
of different perspectives and understandings is essential if the
Church is to grow in self-understanding, and correspondingly
make her gospel relevant to successive generations. Without
diversity she would die.

The word "Catholic," however, penetrates beneath matters

of visible form and organization in another way. It proclaims that universality of the Church's faith which inevitably follows from the fact of one Christ who is the incarnation of the eternal Word of God. He, that is, is the "Alpha and the Omega," the beginning, the end, and all that comes between (Rev. 22:13). In him as "cosmic Christ" is the key to all men's questions and needs.[14] Man's understanding is imperfect, and to look at the history of the Christian Church suggests that there are many "faiths." But "Catholicity" reminds us that such, really, is not the case. For imperfect and fragmented though her witness be, the Church knows but one Christ, and her good news that he is Lord is the same as that which was first shouted almost two thousand years ago.

To mention "sameness," however, is to aver that this "Catholicity" is Apostolic. And this is said explicitly in the longer Nicene Creed: "And I believe one Catholic and *Apostolic* Church." The Church is Apostolic, the Book of Common Prayer states, because "it continues steadfastly in the Apostles' teaching and fellowship."[15] This recalls our own frequent description of the Church's credal formulary as Apostolic Witness, because the Apostles' Creed is a summary of the testimony of those who were there when the first response to things actually seen and heard evolved. And the importance of this "Apostolicity" lies not solely in its reminder of the unbroken continuity of the Catholic faith down through the ages. It

[14] See above, pp. 80–82, 135 f.

[15] The definition of the Church as contained in the Book of Common Prayer, p. 291, is worthy of note because, in its explanation of the relevant credal phrases it adheres closely to the biblical witness:

"We mean that the Church is
  One; because it is one Body under one Head;
  Holy; because the Holy Spirit dwells in it, and sanctifies its members;
  Catholic; because it is universal, holding earnestly the Faith for all time, in all countries, and for all people; and is sent to preach the Gospel to the whole world;
  Apostolic; because it continues stedfastly in the Apostles' teaching and fellowship."

The word "Holy" is discussed below, pp. 198 f.

affirms, as well, that Christian conviction is rooted, not in the speculative endeavor of some erudite intellectual, but in the experience of real people who were irresistibly upturned by knowing Jesus Christ.[16] It reminds us, too, that ultimately Christianity is a life, and not a doctrine, it is personal relationship with others in Christ (the Apostles' "fellowship" in Christ), and not a system of philosophy or ethics, and that the Church's reason for being is to lead people to that same saving knowledge of Jesus as personal Lord which the first eyewitnesses recognized as the one thing of importance in their own lives.

The importance of Christianity's Apostolic origin was something underlined especially in later New Testament times when the Church was beginning to be threatened by anti-historical elements.[17] This was Jude's concern when he wrote of "the faith which was once for all delivered to the saints" (vs. 3). The author of the Pastoral Epistles, also, time and again emphasizes the importance of holding fast to that faith which originated in the earliest days: "Follow the pattern of the sound words which you have heard from me . . . guard the truth that has been entrusted to you"; "continue in what you have learned and have firmly believed"; "teach what befits sound doctrine" (II Tim. 1:13,14; 3:14; Tit. 2:1).[18]

It is the faith of the Apostles to which these writers are referring. The Church, that is, must stand firm on the rock of those who were there when it all began. Only this can be right faith, the Catholic faith. And even though the stress in the above passages is clearly upon a developing system of doctrine, there remains behind it that all-important witness of the very first Christians. "Sound doctrine," Creeds, and, for that matter, preaching, liturgy, sacraments — all have as their purpose the

---

[16] See above, pp. 7–10, 50–59.
[17] Gnosticism, for example, which had a close affinity with Hellenistic dualism (see above, p. 33) tended to look with suspicion upon the material world and historical phenomena. See the note on Docetism, pp. 86–8.
[18] See further I Tim. 3:13, 4:1,6, 6:3,12,20; II Tim. 2:2,15,18; 3:8 ff.; Tit. 1:13 f.

preservation and recalling, for each generation, of the possibility and the reality of sharing in the Apostolic fellowship, which means to live in the community of those who know Jesus the Christ as personal Savior.

There is, then, one faith, and one fellowship, both continuous with the past. But this is also to affirm that only "in the Church" is salvation. To understand this as meaning damnation for all those who are not technically Christians is obvious nonsense, and a travesty of any right understanding of the Church. Wherever one finds the Christ life, wherever one finds the working of that love which denies self in concern for others, there is Christ, and the essence of the Church. God has never for one moment ceased to reveal Himself — and in every place. There *is* only one way to salvation. But to be apprehended by God in Christ does not depend upon one's ability to identify and explain it with the familiar biblical or ecclesiastical labels of the Christian tradition.

True though this is, however, the Church has a missionary mandate. Her life is that of the triangle: God/Christ/Spirit — the Church — the World.[19] If the Church does not give of herself, she dies. And there is this further imperative — the conviction, which she must hold humbly, that specifically to know Jesus of Nazareth is to discern in brightest focus that which God is and wills and does. It is true that God's witness to Himself is present everywhere, and that He can be known in many ways. But there is a great difference between knowing abstract principle on the one hand, and, on the other, concrete historical events and persons. And for Christianity, which is ultimately *personal* relationship, to proclaim the *person* Jesus Christ to those who do not know him, is to make that which is inchoate impellingly real, and to make those things which are intimations rich and fruitful certainties.

God is one who can be intimately known and loved — something which is true of no theory or principle. The Christian

[19] See above, p. 189 f.

194

proclamation is that God who is *person* (and more), and dwells in *personal* relationship with His world, has specifically and supremely and savingly penetrated into people's lives in the one *person* Jesus Christ. This witness in its fullness, the Apostolic Witness, the Catholic faith for all of God's creation — this only the Church preserves and proclaims. Herein lies a chief necessity for her existence as an ecclesiastical organization, and the mandate to proclaim her gospel in all the world.

The Church is further described, in a phrase which appears only in the Apostles' Creed, as "The Communion of Saints." The Greek word *koinōnia* (communion) is a much more powerful term in the biblical idiom than the English translation suggests. It bespeaks sharing, participation, the holding of something to which the group looks back, or a common concern or goal which lies ahead. But in the Church, Christ himself is the common bond. Participation in him is participation one with another, and means a strenuous sharing of self with those others; for Christian life is a being apprehended by love "in the Spirit." As translations of *koinōnia,* then, "communion" and "fellowship" are woefully inadequate. Our best course is to look at the context of its use in the New Testament.

Sometimes the frame of reference for both noun and verb is quite specific and down to earth. Luke, for example, tells us that some early Christians pooled their resources and possessions, and "they had everything in common (*koina*)" (Acts 4:32). Paul frequently refers to the alms which he collected from various Christian communities to help the indigent Jerusalem church as *koinōnia,* that is, "contribution" (Rom. 15:25-29; II Cor. 8:4; 9:13; cf. Heb. 13:16). Such uses are purely "secular," but, even so, important. The bond between individuals and between Christian communities was not simply a "theory," but demanded genuine practical concern, precisely of the sort illustrated by these uses of *koinōnia,* for others.

Closely related is the use of the same word in general ethical contexts. "If we say," writes the author of I John, "we have *koinōnia* with [Christ] while we walk in darkness, we lie and do not live according to the truth" (1:6). In other words, union with Christ is a mandate for giving of self (love) to others: "This I command you, to love one another" (John 15:17). To be "in Christ," and yet to disregard one's neighbor — these are irreconcilable opposites (I John 3:17; 4:20).[20]

This word, too, has a doctrinal orientation. The opening verses of I John, for example, remind the readers of the Church's fundamental gospel. The earthly Jesus ("That . . . which we have heard, which we have seen with our eyes . . . and touched with our hands") is the pre-existent divine Logos ("which was from the beginning . . . the word of life"). This, he goes on to say, we "proclaim also to you, so that you may have fellowship (*koinōnia*) with us" (I John 1:1–4; cf. Pm. 6). Here is the same pattern which we noted as underlying our Creeds: God and Christ are proclaimed (Articles 1, 2); the response of faith is given (Article 3).[21] In the text before us, actually, the result of faith is given, "fellowship," that is, life as Christian community. Life as Church, and loving relationship with others, are rooted in a common and right faith in Jesus Christ.

There is still one final use of the word *koinōnia:*

> The cup of blessing which we bless, is it not a participation [*koinōnia*] in the blood of Christ? The bread which we break, is it not a participation in the body of Christ? Because there is one loaf, we who are many are one body, for we all partake of the same loaf (I Cor. 10:16,17).

Here we have one of Paul's two explicit references to the Church's Eucharist. The other occurs in the very next chapter, I Corinthians 11:17-34. It is perhaps not mere chance that

[20] See above, pp. 186 f.
[21] See above, pp. 158 f.

these both appear immediately prior to the Apostle's first and most graphic description of the Church as the Body of Christ in chapter 12. Nor is it accidental that each occurs in a context denouncing certain sins of the readers which are splitting the community at Corinth into many tiny factions. Let us recall that with which the Eucharist began.

The Last Supper on the night of the betrayal was a climactic sharing between Jesus and his own of all that he was, the sealing of a new and binding covenant. The life of the Kingdom is the Christ life of death to self in order to fulfill self in loving relationship with others. And so this last meal together was the founding of the new people of God, the one Body of Christ.[22]

Paul's Eucharistic references, and particularly his use of *koinōnia* in the text cited above, stand out in sharp relief against the shattering unloving factionalism which so distresses him. Divisiveness — this was the chief note of the Corinthian community. Yet the Church is *one* Body, a "fellowship" of each with the other, because all alike are "in Christ" and equal recipients of his love. And Paul understands the Eucharist — and this is why he speaks of it here, and in the way in which he does — as the supreme expression of the Church's *oneness*. Every time the bread is broken, it is a renewal of the binding covenant which created the one Church on the eve of Good Friday, and the renewal for each individual present of that *koinōnia* which had begun for him at his baptism.

The breaking of bread, we noted, is the recalling (*anamnēsis*) of Christ's death and Resurrection, and the most dramatic outward enactment of the triangle life — for here together are Christ, Everyman, and his neighbor. In her Eucharistic action, the Church as Christ's Body for a few brief moments actually lives that which she strives to be and to make a reality at every time and in every place. Here she is most truly herself, and her members most vividly realize what salvation is and can be.

[22] See above, pp. 166–9.

197

What does it mean to say that the Church is "Holy," that all Christians are "Saints"? Not sinless, perfect — at least so far as the New Testament use of the words is concerned. Paul, for example, speaks of all Christians at Corinth as "saints." But the most superficial reading of his letters makes it perfectly clear that few if any of his readers were candidates for sainthood by present-day criteria.

The term "saint" comes from the Greek adjective *hagios* (holy). This word, like the corresponding Hebrew *qadosh*, designates first of all a thing or a person which has been dedicated to that which alone is holy, God. So Leviticus 19:2 reads, "You shall be holy; for I the Lord your God am holy." Here holiness results from the fact that Israel has been chosen, called, covenanted by God. And the basic meaning of the term is "holy because set apart for that which is holy."

This, predominantly, is the New Testament usage. Repeatedly we find the phrase "called to be saints" (I Cor. 1:2). This is precisely equivalent to the phrase "called to be Jesus Christ's" (Rom. 1:6). That is, "saint" and "Christian" mean the same thing. Members of the Church are those who have answered God's call, been set apart as His people, had their lives radically changed because now the center is not self, but Christ. Not perfection, then, but deep personal commitment to the life of the Kingdom is the essence of sainthood. The old adage, "a saint is a sinner who keeps on trying," contains not a little truth. For the Christian is one who recognizes and answers God's sovereign call, knows that he cannot go it alone, accepts the forgiveness of the cross, and moves on. Sainthood is a striving "in Christ" unto salvation.

The Church, then, as "The Communion of Saints" is holy because her life, however imperfect, is grounded in God's call and God's purpose and God's command. Aware of her imperfections, she knows her need, and God's power to make up her deficiencies. Would that she were perfect. But that attitude which will have nothing to do with the Church (or with a particular parish) because her members so obviously fall short of their calling is both unrealistic and unbiblical.

"I believe in the Holy Catholic Church, the Communion of Saints." The best commentary upon this credal affirmation is to be found in these familiar words:

> There is one body and one Spirit, just as you were called to the one hope that belongs to your call, one Lord, one faith, one baptism, one God and Father of us all, who is above all and through all and in all (Eph. 4:4-6).

Here we have a moving summary of salvation as a process of becoming.

The Church is not perfect, but Holy — because she has been called to that which is holy, and is rooted in that which is holy, God in Christ.

The Church is Catholic, and one Body in Christ — because she has one Lord, one faith, one baptism, and, let us add, one Eucharist.

The Church is a people of God which is a Communion, a Fellowship of Saints — because her members recognize, however dimly, their need, see in Jesus the Christ the answer to that need, believe that in the life of dependence upon God and love for neighbor is to be found full selfhood. In baptism they have answered God's call. In Eucharist they briefly know the full meaningfulness of saved lives. And the reality which they find in all this (indeed God has poured the Spirit of the last days into our lives!) leads them to look ahead not only with awe, but also with unshakable hope.

VI

Resurrection of the Body, Life
Everlasting — Salvation as Future

The early Christian hoped for salvation.

True, at one moment he thought of himself as already saved by virtue of his baptism. And in the breaking of bread he glimpsed again and again the glory and the wonder of that which could be. Still, facts were facts. Jesus would return, and "we must all appear before the judgment seat of Christ" (II Cor. 5:10; cf. Rom. 14:10).

Furthermore, day to day growing unto salvation proved to be no easy matter. Faith is hard work, love is toil, hope demands fortitude (I Th. 1:3). Moreover, to faith and hope there is a decided risk; it is to stake one's future on intangibles. After all, "hope that is seen is not hope"; and "faith is the assurance of things hoped for, the conviction of things not seen" (Rom. 8:24; Heb. 11:1). Paul was right when he said that one must work out his salvation "with fear and trembling" (Phil. 2:12).

Nevertheless — a paradox, to be sure — the Christian hope for future salvation was a sure hope. These words give a hint of how this could be:

> More than that, we rejoice in our sufferings, knowing that suffering produces endurance, and endurance produces character, and character produces hope, and hope does not disappoint us, because God's love has been poured into our hearts through the Holy Spirit which has been given to us (Rom. 5:3–5).

Astounding words, these: *"rejoice* in our sufferings"! This is really to turn things upside down. The Apostle says the same thing elsewhere: "I will all the more gladly boast of my weaknesses . . . I am content with weaknesses, insults, hardships, persecutions, and calamities; for when I am weak, then I am strong" (II Cor. 12:9,10).

But this was precisely the scandal of the cross — that it is in the midst of deepest weakness and humiliation that there comes one's greatest exaltation (I Cor. 1:18–31). And this was perhaps the most startling thing about the newness of these Christian lives — that adverse circumstances *strengthened* courage and joy and hope. In other words, and to be frankly pragmatic about it, their faith worked. They had received the Spirit; God through His Messiah had as never before entered into their lives. They knew it to be true.

So their faith was not an illusion, not mere wishful thinking — for it did not "disappoint" them. It was sheer fact, that hope for the present — for life with meaning and joy — proved itself every day. How could the same hope for the future turn out to be illusory? What God had so richly done was irresistibly real, and He was powerful to finish it — both for the world, and for them. Salvation was assured.

Judgment there would be, and the first believers took this seriously. Sin was still a part of their lives, and this could not be without consequence. There are illogicalities here, of course: they had been saved, they feared judgment, they knew forgiveness, they alternated between fear and hope. But this does not mean that what they said was untrue — nor any part of it. The whole thing was simply beyond them, too great for human logicality. Often, the whole truth can be expressed only in paradox.

How did this sure hope for future salvation express itself? The New Testament speaks chiefly in terms of Parousia, resurrection of the dead, judgment, and final condemnation or felicity. Parousia and judgment we have already discussed in connection with the final affirmation of the second Article.[1]

[1] See above, pp. 143–53.

We turn now to resurrection, and life everlasting.

Future salvation meant "Resurrection of the body."

Here Christianity has inherited from a complicated background of Jewish speculation. It was not until the last two or three centuries immediately before Christ that the Hebraic concept of a future life, hitherto so vague and amorphous as to be all but meaningless, began to express itself in more concrete terms. For the moment we need consider but one aspect — the belief that, at the time of the catastrophic end of the world, the graves would be opened so that both "quick and dead" might be judged, some happily to share in God's new creation.

In its earliest Christian form, the resurrection hope was literalistic and vivid. Paul's description of those both living and dead being "caught up . . . in the clouds to meet the Lord in the air" is typical of the imaginings of most believers (I Th. 4:17). The same literalism is illustrated by Matthew's tale of an earthquake which opened the tombs in Jerusalem at the moment of Jesus' death, so that after his Resurrection many of the dead wandered about the holy city (27:51-54). Passages such as these reflect Christian borrowing from Judaism's picture of last-day phenomena, the same source that provided much of the language employed by the primitive Church to detail Jesus' Parousia, and the judgment scenes in which he plays a central role.[2]

The Christian future hope, as we have already suggested, may not have crystallized immediately.[3] At first Jesus' followers simply waited for the cataclysmic end of all things. But as delay continued, expectant believers died; and then the matter of resurrection in order to share in the joys of that which was still future became something of poignant importance.

[2] See above, pp. 143-52, where the close relationship between such language, and Judaism's Son of Man expectation, is detailed.
[3] See above, p. 148.

It was this circumstance, for example, that was distressing the new converts in Thessalonica. Already, in the few months since Paul had preached there, and proclaimed Jesus' imminent return, a few had died. Did this mean that these, through sheer bad luck, had lost out? Surely not, he answers: "For since we believe that Jesus died and rose again, even so, through Jesus, God will bring with him those who have fallen alseep" (I Th. 4:14). The author of the Fourth Gospel puts it this way: "I am the resurrection and the life; he who believes in me, though he die, yet shall he live" (11:25).

These last two quotations make it clear that the Christian hope was indigenous. From Judaism came much of the imagery with which the last things were pictured. But it was Jesus' own Resurrection which ultimately impelled the Church's certainty in this matter. So, to Christians in Corinth, Paul writes, "Now if Christ is preached as raised from the dead, how can some of you say that there is no resurrection of the dead?" (15:12). Jesus is "the first-born from the dead," and "the first fruits of those who have fallen asleep" (Col. 1:18; I Cor. 15:20). "If the Spirit of him who raised Jesus from the dead dwells in you, he who raised Christ Jesus from the dead will give life to your mortal bodies also through his Spirit which dwells in you" (Rom. 8:11).

The last of these texts points to another important aspect of the resurrection hope. It is, Paul writes, God's Spirit which will raise the Christian. This same Spirit, moreover, is that which raised Jesus, and which now dominates one's present life. It is not, then, just the Resurrection of Jesus, but equally the believer's apprehension and living of the powerfully new resurrection life "in Christ" *now*, which makes for such surety with respect to the future. In this way, too, the Christian hope is indigenous. First in baptism, then repeatedly in the breaking of bread, and in his day-by-day living as well, one knows the startling joy of life welcomed as a gift of God's sovereign love — so much so that it is simply inconceivable that life can either be in vain or come to nought. "For if we have been united with him in a death like his, we shall certainly be united with him in a resurrection like his" — not just now, but in the future, and for all eternity (Rom. 6:5).

In contrast to the literalism of the popular hope, it is important at this point to recall the evidence that Paul had thought deeply on this matter, and in his letters spoke of a concept of bodily resurrection which, at least in germ, was far less materialistic than that of most of his subsequent interpreters.[4] He strongly underlined the "otherness" of life beyond the grave: "I tell you this, brethren: flesh and blood cannot inherit the kingdom of God, nor does the perishable inherit the imperishable" (I Cor. 15:50). But, there must be some form of embodiment: "For we know that if the earthly tent we live in [the fleshly body of this life] is destroyed, we have a building from God, a house not made with hands, eternal in the heavens" (II Cor. 5:1). And yet, "this mortal nature must put on immortality" (I Cor. 15:53). So, on the one hand, Paul can speak of Christian longing for the future in terms of "redemption of our bodies" (Rom. 8:23). But to his readers at Philippi, he writes with perfect equanimity of dying before the Parousia and, without any concern for a bodily last-day resurrection, of being immediately with Christ (Phil. 1:19–26).

All in all, may well be baffled by the seeming confusion here. But the fact of the matter is that the future life is something quite beyond man's imagining, and the Apostle, one suspects, realized this. Here, as we suggested earlier, is warning against any overly literalistic interpretation of the descriptive imagery which we may use in this connection.[5] And there is certainly biblical justification for taking exception to some early forms of our Creeds which affirmed "the resurrection of the flesh."[6] And what of the phrase in the Nicene Creed,

[4] See above, pp. 109–12.
[5] See above, pp. 138 f.
[6] See, for example, the "Old Roman Creed" cited in Appendix II.

affirmation "Resurrection of the *body*" in the Apostles' Creed?

This latter suggestion must not be embraced too hastily. For Paul has something else to say, perhaps the most important thing of all — there is between this life and the next an essential continuity. Here we recall his analogy of the seed:

> But some one will ask, "How are the dead raised? With what kind of body do they come?" You foolish man! What you sow does not come to life unless it dies. And what you sow is not the body which is to be, but a bare kernel, perhaps of wheat or of some other grain. But God gives it a body as he has chosen, and to each kind of seed its own body (I Cor. 15:35-38).

That there is an identity between this life and that beyond the grave is apparent.

Paul's next words in this same context underline the difference between the two states. There are many kinds of flesh, that of men and beasts and birds and fish. There are, too, different kinds of bodies, celestial and terrestrial; and sun, moon, and stars each have their own peculiar "glories" (vss. 39-41). Even here, however, the idea of embodiment remains as a constant, and in the next block of verses he returns to the seed analogy:

> So it is with the resurrection of the dead. What is sown is perishable, what is raised is imperishable. It is sown in dishonor, it is raised in glory. It is sown in weakness, it is raised in power. It is sown a physical body, it is raised a spiritual body. If there is a physical body, there is also a spiritual body (vss. 42-44).

[7] The phrase in the Nicene Creed recalls the New Testament practice of referring to Jesus' Resurrection as "from among the dead." See above, p. 117.

In these verses both truths are underlined. The "otherness" is stressed by the contrasts "perishable — imperishable," "physical body — spiritual body." At the same time, there can be no mistaking the stress upon the "sameness" which connects the "before" and "after." [8]

It has been important to detail this at some length. For Paul's insight here opens the way to a realistic and profoundly meaningful understanding of the credal phrase "Resurrection of the body."

Hellenistic thought conceived of man as composed of two parts — the fleshly body, and the soul. Only the latter was really significant. It was temporarily encased in the body, and at death escaped this prison to go on to some kind of vague future existence called "immortality." [9] This view is not without its value. Paul himself, for example, underlines the fact that the present form of corporeal existence is temporary, and something which will be sloughed off. And the Hellenistic concept of immortality points to something else that the Apostle stresses — that the future life is existence of a dimension totally other than that which we know at present. But the vagueness of it all has no reality for us. We simply can't imagine "bodiless-ness." It goes against the grain. In contrast, however, the Jewish-Christian concept goes *with* the grain.

The Hebraic doctrine of man made no sharp distinction between body and soul. Body and spirit, yes — the latter in the sense of life, or the breath of life which is given by God, and animates. But when that spirit departs, then the body dies, and "personhood" in any meaningful sense simply no longer exists. When, as we noted earlier, late Judaism began to concentrate more upon the after life, she thought in terms of a re-

[8] According to the Fourth Gospel, Jesus says, "Truly, truly, I say to you, unless a grain of wheat falls into the earth and dies, it remains alone; but if it dies, it bears much fruit. He who loves his life loses it, and he who hates his life in this world will keep it for eternal life" (12:24,25). This reminder of the seed analogy in I Corinthians suggests that John, too, may have understood resurrection as a "non-fleshly" phenomenon. See below, p. 213.
[9] See above, p. 33.

embodiment of that shadowy existence which wandered color-lessly in the place of departed shades.[10] In other words, not the spirit (soul) alone, but the body as well, was essential to significant existence. Without the latter, there cannot be a real person.

For this reason, then, life beyond the grave of necessity involved bodily resurrection. And it is this doctrine of man and this concept of the future, rather than the Hellenistic idiom of immortality, which is the core of the Christian hope. But Paul, who shares in this heritage, at the same time intuitively recognizes that the Jewish idiom is a metaphorical expression of an essential truth. Future life is something completely different from the present human circumstance. That there should be literal reconstitution of the same flesh he knows to be irrelevant. But even so, the Apostle is aware that the essence of the Hebraic understanding is of singular importance, and he retains it by use of that seed analogy which stresses the continuity which exists between the "before" and the "after."

There is nothing in Paul's recorded words to suggest how, if at all, he had worked it out in his own mind. But the implications of what he does tell us can be discerned. Between one's body and one's total self there is a relationship which is not transient and incidental, but *essential*. This signifies that the whole self, although it is more than the earthly body, cannot, as long as it is the same meaningful self, be without that body. And the credal phrase, "Resurrection of the body," proclaims that future life does not represent a loss, but is a fuller meaningful continuance of that whole self.

This does not, however, require that we postulate the reconstitution of the same earthly flesh. For life beyond the grave is quite another dimension of existence. Rather, the essential relationship between body and self which we have just underlined means that everything about present corporeal existence — every concrete and inconcrete reality which one encounters —

[10] See above, pp. 137 f.

makes an individual what he is, comes to be a part of him. A person becomes who and what he is out of the matrix of everything that the human phenomenal circumstance involves. And this, all of it, as it were, stays with him. It remains, that is, indispensable to that self which is now in process of becoming, and which, in the life beyond, continues on to that perfect wholeness which is salvation. And when the actual moment comes to move from one sphere of existence to another, it is this total self that "rises."

This, admittedly, is to say little that is specific about life after death. The Christian, however, because he believes that the future is essentially and meaningfully continuous with what he experiences in the present, boldly says, "In the life beyond the grave, we will know and be known by those whom we love, and by those who love us; for all that they were and are, has been, and remains, integral to what we are, and shall be." [11] Need one, really, know more? This is the kind of sure hope which lies behind the words "Resurrection of the body," and which makes them preferable to the Nicene Creed's less precise "Resurrection of the dead."

And all this is because of Christ, and "in Christ." To know him in this present world is to be gripped now and here by the power of his Resurrection. Death-Resurrection had been the shape of Jesus' own life in its entirety (death to self for God and others), so that, as we look back, the climactic Good Friday weekend of complete loss and a God-given newness seems almost inevitable. So it is for the person who is Christ's in this present world. Death-Resurrection for the believer proves itself as life from above. Here, it is a becoming, a struggle unto salvation; for death to the wrong kind of self is slow and painful. But hope for the future is sure because one's hope for each present moment is so often fulfilled. Faith "in Christ" *is* something utterly and convincingly different from the life of "unfaith." There will come the time, beyond the grave, when

[11] See above, p. 115.

208

that full selfhood of which now one has but glimpses will exist in all its God-intended glory.[12] This is salvation, begun in baptism, long in coming, but at last a full reality.

In the chronological scheme of things, resurrection of the dead served a very practical purpose. One must be raised in order to stand before the throne of judgment and be consigned to everlasting torment or bliss. Furthermore, as we have seen, the biblical commentary on this concept says important things about the nature of life beyond the grave. The credal phrase "the Life everlasting" speaks to this future in another way.

Something that goes on and on *ad infinitum* — this is the picture conjured up by the words "everlasting" and "eternal." And some who find this thought wearisome may prefer the alternative offered by the Nicene Creed: "the Life of the world to come." More important, however, is the fact that this longer and more descriptive phrase reflects with greater clarity Jesus' own teaching with respect to future life.

In Hebraic thought, at the time of Christian origins, life beyond the grave meant life in the Kingdom of God. This was a basic premise of Judaism's future hope. Resurrection, we recall, was one of the phenomena which would accompany the catastrophic arrival of that Kingdom. And the ensuing new life (which was frequently spoken of as "life eternal," because God's consummation of history would surely stand forever) would, for the righteous, be a sharing in all the joys of God's new creation. Judaism, therefore, often termed that future "the life of the age to come," a manner of expression which points, not to extent of time, but to the contrast between the present age or world which man experiences now, and that drastically other existence under God's total sovereignty. Not duration,

[12] One may well suspect that such fullness is not attained immediately. Must not the process of growth unto salvation continue in one's new state of existence? See below, p. 214 f.

then, but the fact of a new kind of life, was the chief point of emphasis.

Both of our credal phrases, "Life of the world (*aiōn*) to come" and "the life everlasting (*aiōnios*)," occur in the New Testament. And without ignoring the fact that time without end is a part of the biblical meaning, it is important to remember the underlying Hebraic background which we outlined above. Here a look at the original Greek is helpful. *Aiōn* means "world," "age," and, secondarily, "eternity." *Aiōnios* is translated "eternal," "everlasting"; but this latter, for Judaism, meant "the life of eternity," the life, that is, of "the age to come." There is striking illustration of this in Mark 10:30, where Jesus, after having spoken of entrance into God's Kingdom, refers to the final benefit with the words "and in the *aiōn* to come life *aiōnios*." And these representative texts also underline the fact that "eternity" means much more than simply endless duration:

> . . . but whoever speaks against the Holy Spirit will not be forgiven, either in this age or in the age to come (Matt. 12:32).

> "Good Teacher, what must I do to inherit eternal life?" . . . And Jesus looked around and said to his disciples, "How hard it will be for those who have riches to enter the kingdom of God!" (Mark 10:17-23; cf. Luke 10:25-28).

The first text reminds us that Jesus spoke repeatedly, in the Hebraic idiom, of the two periods or ages of history. In the second, the parallelism of verses 17 and 23 demanded by the context shows that "eternal life" means the life of the Kingdom, which, as we have seen, is to speak primarily of a quality of existence.

Duration of time, then, is but one facet of a much broader concept. It was, of course, the imminence of that coming age upon which Jesus' ministry centered, and its meaningfulness in terms of new life which his words and works made so real to the eyewitnesses. And it was this same "qualitative" aspect of existence under God, both present and future, that was his chief concern. Not bliss monotonously going on and on forever, but the revolutionary newness and otherness of that kind of life which truly welcomes God's reign — this was the focal point of Jesus' teaching.

But what can we say of the idea of unending time? This is a part of the biblical concept of eternity. Actually, it may be helpful to remember, time is an earth-bound concept, a way which we have of expressing one of the limitations of the human circumstance. Paradoxically, we suggest that "everlasting" underlines the fact that life beyond the grave will not be subject to the frustrating "ups" and "downs" of our present transient existence. It points, that is, to something which is inconceivable to us now, namely, "timelessness." And the phrase in the Nicene Creed, "the Life of the world to come," reminds us that there lies ahead not a barren "without end," but an inexhaustible fullness of the wondrousness which we all glimpse, but briefly, in this world: "For now we see in a mirror dimly, but then face to face. Now I know in part; then I shall understand fully, even as I have been fully understood" (I Cor. 13:12). To recognize this is to look forward to the future with joy.

One of the things stressed repeatedly in the pages of this study has been the fact that confession of God and Christ as proclaimed in the first two Articles of the Creed involves risk. In the very nature of the case, one cannot prove that the Christian interpretation of that which occurred "under Pontius Pilate" was and is the correct one. As a corollary to this, we have spoken much of Christian experience, and asserted that ultimately faith has to authenticate itself in the lives of those who are willing to take the risk.[13] Particularly, the matter of

[13] See above, p. 11.

the future hope, which has been our recent concern, illustrates the point. It is, we noted, because one's own longing for meaningful existence in each present moment is fulfilled, that there is such certainty with respect to what lies ahead.[14]

But Article Three as a whole underlines this same frankly pragmatic aspect of the Christian faith. For, as we stated earlier, the things which it proclaims, Spirit, Church, Salvation, were initially not so much matters formally confessed, but realities which happened to those who accepted Jesus as the Christ of God.[15] And it was the resultant transformed lives of those first believers which confirmed their new commitment, and moulded it into an unshakable faith which made formal confession possible. Today, also, this third Article points to the kind of life which the Christian knows to be possible because, however imperfectly, it is his own. And formal confession of this life in the Creed is the Church's public avowal that this, and no other, is God's way and demand and promise for the world of men, and her invitation to come and learn for one's self what it means to see Him in the face of Jesus Christ.

Let us turn briefly to the writer of the Fourth Gospel. This Evangelist has done interesting things with the primitive tradition about the future hope, and in the process speaks clearly to the experiential element of a Christian faith which proves itself in daily living.

In the first place, John is not overly interested in the chronological scheme of the last things. He nods to the Parousia tradition; and yet, for him, the return of Christ has, to all intents and purposes, already occurred. In one text, for example, Jesus says, "And I will pray the Father, and he will give you another Counselor, to be with you forever" (14:16). But in the next verse but one, he adds, "I will not leave you desolate; *I* will come to you" (vs. 18).[16] "Counselor," often termed

[14] See above, pp. 201, 203 f.
[15] See above, p. 159.
[16] See also 14:23,28; 16:16, etc. (Italics mine.)

"Paraclete" or "Comforter," is John's way of referring to the Holy Spirit. For this Evangelist, Christ through the Spirit is already fully present with his Church.[17]

John, too, knows the Church's tradition with respect to resurrection at the last day, and final judgment: "for the hour is coming when all who are in the tombs will hear his voice and come forth, those who have done good, to the resurrection of life, and those who have done evil, to the resurrection of judgment" (5:28,29). And yet, repeatedly throughout his Gospel he points to eternal life as a possession that one has *now*. This is nowhere more graphically stated than in 11:25,26: "I am the resurrection and the life; he who believes in me, though he die, yet shall he live, and whoever lives and believes in me shall never die" (cf. 3:36; 5:24; etc.). That is, in each present moment, rightly understood and embraced, one finds the reassurance that life "under God" is an irrevocable gift.

Judgment, too, is *now;* acceptance or condemnation are present experiences determined by one's acceptance or rejection of Christ: "He who believes in him is not condemned; he who does not believe is condemned already, because he has not believed in the name of the only Son of God" (3:18). In other words, the Johannine perspective sees the resurrection and judgment of the last day as but a final sealing of that which the individual Christian is and does with his daily life. All that the traditional future hope points to is tellingly real *now* — for condemnation and blessing are inseparable parts of every circumstance and every decision that one faces. Not, that is, just in some vague future, but every moment now is bright with promise.

John's stress upon the present world is deeply meaningful. And yet, it could be said that his tendency to minimize the traditional future hope is a loss. In the picture of the Parousia and all that goes with it, we have a dramatic underlining of an

---

[17] We recall here the close association between the Resurrection of Jesus and the Spirit. See above, pp. 105 f.

integral element of the basic Christian gospel, one which is weighty with significance — that all things are inescapably moving with purpose toward a goal, God's End, and that "in Christ" man's own reason for being is sure, and a part of that divine purpose.[18] This is important, and an accent much needed. For, as the first Christians knew, life in this world with its frustrations and limitations can at times seem like a ceaseless round of futility.

At the same time, John and Paul alike bear witness to this fact — that the Christian's *now* in faith is so convincingly different from the life of "unfaith" that even in the midst of the greatest stresses he knows that heaven begins here on earth.

Let us put it — and finally so — this way. There is, the Christian knows, future salvation because he knows salvation now. There is judgment to come, because he knows what it is to stand under judgment now. There is a resurrection (and Christ must have been raised!) because "in Christ" he knows what it is to be risen now. That which is yet to come beyond the grave will be "selfhood" in a meaningful and recognizable sense, because to be a person now, although still in painful process of becoming, is so precious a gift. And heaven there must be, too, because this also the believer knows as inescapable present reality.

And what of hell? This is present reality, too. The inevitable result of refusing to let God reign is hell. But what of life beyond the grave?

This we must say. The life which has not learned here to let God reign will hardly be content in heaven where God's will *is* done. The struggle unto salvation — and will this not be true for all to some degree? — will have to go on. But is it really conceivable that any life can resist its Creator forever?

The heart of God's relationship with His world is love. And love is first and foremost a dynamic, the creative and re-creative power of God omnipotent. Even human lives, as we at one

[18] See above, pp. 152 f.

point suggested, give us a hint.[19] It is possible, and it does happen — that there can be a love so stubborn and persistent, so penetrating, that eventually the beloved can no longer resist.

Nor is this a denial or curtailing of the beloved's freedom not to love, something, of course, which there must be as a genuine alternative if love is to have any meaning. Eventually the beloved responds, voluntarily, freely — and there is joy.

We do not, then, go on to discuss everlasting damnation as an alternative to everlasting life.[20] And our two Creeds say nothing of such a possibility. This may be mere chance, historical coincidence — or it may be Providence!

[19] See above, p. 131.
[20] See above, pp. 138 f.

215

Appendix I

The order of the various books in the canonical New Testament is quite independent of their date of composition. Although many uncertainties remain, the probable dates of writing are as follows:

? Galatians	A.D. 48-50 ?
I Thessalonians	50
II Thessalonians	50-51
I Corinthians II Corinthians Galatians	52-54
? Colossians ? Philippians ? Philemon	52-54?
Romans	55-56
Colossians Philippians Philemon	60-62
Gospel of Mark	65-75
James Ephesians	75-100

Gospel of Luke }	
Acts }	85-100
Gospel of Matthew }	
I Peter }	
Hebrews }	90-95
Revelation }	
Gospel of John }	
I, II, III John }	90-110
I Timothy }	
II Timothy }	100-130
Titus }	
Jude	110-130
II Peter	130-150

It should be noted further that the Authorized Version's ascription of Hebrews to the Apostle Paul is erroneous, and that the majority of scholars are dubious as to the Pauline authorship of the Pastorals (I, II Timothy, Titus), and of Ephesians. Some scholars have similar doubts with respect to Colossians and II Thessalonians.

The Mark responsible for the Gospel which bears his name may have been the John Mark who was at one time associated with Paul (Acts 12:25; 13:13; Col. 4:10; Pm. 24; II Tim. 4:11; cf. Acts 12:12; 15:37-40). There is a tradition that he was closely associated with Peter in Rome, and some of the materials in his Gospel may be Petrine reminiscences (I Pt. 5:13).

That the Apostles Matthew (Mark 3:18; Matt. 10:3; Luke 6:15; Acts 1:13) and John, the son of Zebedee, were to any substantial degree responsible for the Gospels which bear their names is highly unlikely. The other son of Zebedee, the Apostle James, was martyred by Herod Agrippa I, King of Palestine A.D. 41-44 (Acts 12:1-3). It is possible, however, that the James

218

who was the brother of Jesus (Matt. 13:55; Mark 6:3; Gal. 1:19, etc.) is responsible for the brief book which bears this name.

Jude is a pseudonymous reference to Judas, another brother of Jesus (Matt. 13:55; Mark 6:3). Second Peter and, in all probability, I Peter as well, are likewise pseudonymous. Peter (and perhaps Paul, as well) was martyred in Rome, perhaps in connection with the Neronian persecution of A.D. 64.

Appendix II

The "Old Roman Creed" can be traced back to the closing decades of the second Christian century. It was a local creed which was employed in connection with the baptismal rite of the Church in Rome. The Latin text is preserved for us in Tyrannius Rufinus' "Commentarius in symbolum apostolorum," which he wrote at the beginning of the fifth century. An English translation follows:

> I believe in God the Father Almighty:
> And in Christ Jesus his only Son, our Lord: Who was born from the Holy Ghost and the Virgin Mary: Who under Pontius Pilate was crucified and buried: On the third day he rose again from the dead: He ascended into Heaven, And sits on the right hand of the Father: From thence he shall come to judge the quick and the dead.
> And in the Holy Ghost: The holy Church: The remission of sins: The Resurrection of the flesh.

Appendix III

The Nicene Creed was formulated at the Council of Nicaea, from which it takes its name and which was held in A.D. 325. It was the first Creed to be used by the entire Church, both East and West. It was revised and finally, in the form presently used, promulgated by the Council of Constantinople in 381. The text follows:

I believe in one God the Father Almighty, Maker of heaven and earth, And of all things visible and invisible:

And in one Lord Jesus Christ, the only-begotten Son of God; Begotten of his Father before all worlds, God of God, Light of Light, Very God of very God; Begotten, not made; Being of one substance with the Father; By whom all things were made: Who for us men and for our salvation came down from heaven, And was incarnate by the Holy Ghost of the Virgin Mary, And was made man: And was crucified also for us under Pontius Pilate; He suffered and was buried: And the third day he rose again according to the Scriptures: And ascended into heaven, And sitteth on the right hand of the Father: And he shall come again, with glory, to judge both the quick and the dead; Whose kingdom shall have no end.

And I believe in the Holy Ghost, The Lord, and Giver of Life, Who proceedeth from the Father and the Son; Who with the Father and the Son together is worshipped and glorified; Who spake by the Prophets: And I believe one Catholic and Apostolic Church: I acknowledge one Baptism for the remission of sins: And I look for the Resurrection of the dead: And the Life of the world to come. Amen.

Bibliography

For those who wish to do further reading, the following recent books on the creeds and fundamental Christian beliefs may prove helpful:

Bethune-Baker, James F. *The Faith of the Apostles' Creed*. Abridged and edited by W. Norman Pittenger. Greenwich: Seabury, 1955.

Brunner, Emil. *I Believe in God: Sermons on the Apostles' Creed*. Translated and edited by John Holden. Philadelphia: Westminster, 1961.

Burnaby, John. *The Belief of Christendom: A Commentary on the Nicene Creed*. London: S.P.C.K., 1960.

Day, Gardiner M. *The Apostles' Creed: An Interpretation for Today*. New York: Scribners, 1963.

Grant, Frederick C. *Basic Christian Beliefs*. Edinburgh and London: Oliver and Boyd Ltd., 1960.

Lampe, G. W. H. *I Believe*. London: Skeffington and Son Ltd., 1960.

Pike, James A., and Pittenger, W. Norman. *The Faith of the Church*. Greenwich: Seabury, 1956.

Robinson, John A. T. *Honest to God*. Philadelphia: Westminster, 1963.

Vidler, Alec R. *Christian Belief: An Exposition of the Basic Christian Doctrines*. London: SCM Press Ltd., 1957.

Whale, J. S. *Christian Doctrine*. London and Glasgow: Collins Clear-Type Press, 1958.

Wilder, Amos N. *New Testament Faith for Today*. New York: Harper, 1955.

The following, representative of various areas of current biblical scholarship, are equally rewarding:

I. THE OLD TESTAMENT

Anderson, B. W. *Understanding the Old Testament*. Englewood Cliffs: Prentice-Hall, Inc., 1957.

Guthrie, Harvey H. *God and History in the Old Testament*. Greenwich: Seabury, 1960.

II. THE ENVIRONMENT OF CHRISTIAN ORIGINS

Cross, Frank M. *The Ancient Library of Qumran and Modern Biblical Studies.* Garden City: Doubleday, 1958.

Grant, Frederick C. *Ancient Judaism and the New Testament.* New York: Macmillan, 1959.

Grant, Frederick C. *Roman Hellenism and the New Testament.* New York: Scribners, 1963.

III. THE LIFE AND TEACHING OF JESUS

Beare, Frank W. *The Earliest Records of Jesus.* New York: Abingdon, 1962. ('An especially interesting commentary on the gospels of Matthew, Mark, and Luke.)

Bethune-Baker, James F. *Early Traditions About Jesus.* Abridged and edited by W. Norman Pittenger. Greenwich: Seabury, 1956.

Bornkamm, Günther. *Jesus of Nazareth.* Translated by Irene and Fraser McLuskey with James M. Robinson. New York: Harper, 1960.

Dibelius, Martin. *Jesus.* Translated by Charles B. Hedrick and Frederick C. Grant. Philadelphia: Westminster, 1949.

Enslin, Morton S. *The Prophet from Nazareth.* New York: McGraw-Hill, 1961.

Grant, Frederic C. "Jesus Christ," *The Interpreter's Dictionary of the Bible.* New York: Abingdon, 1962. Vol. 2, pp. 869 ff.

Johnson, Sherman E. *Jesus in His Homeland.* New York: Scribners, 1957.

Taylor, Vincent. *The Life and Ministry of Jesus.* New York: Abingdon, 1955.

IV. THE LIFE, FAITH, AND LITERATURE OF THE NEW TESTAMENT CHURCH

Dibelius, Martin. *A Fresh Approach to the New Testament and Early Christian Literature.* New York: Scribners, 1936.

Dibelius, Martin. *Paul.* Edited by W. G. Kümmel. Philadelphia: Westminster, 1953.

Grant, Frederick C. *An Introduction to New Testament Thought.* New York: Abingdon-Cokesbury, 1950.

Grant, Frederick C. *The Gospels: Their Origin and Their Growth.* New York: Harper, 1957.

Grant, Robert M. *A Historical Introduction to the New Testament.* New York: Harper, 1963.

Hunter, Archibald M. *Introducing the New Testament.* London: SCM Press Ltd., 1957 (second edition).

Knox, John. *The Church and the Reality of Christ*. New York: Harper, 1962.

Knox, John. *The Death of Christ: The Cross in New Testament History and Faith*. New York: Abingdon, 1958.

Stewart, James. *A Man in Christ*. New York: Harper, 1935.

V. GENERAL REFERENCE WORKS

Hasting, James. *Dictionary of the Bible*. Revised by F. C. Grant and H. H. Rowley. New York: Scribners, 1963 (second edition).

The Interpreter's Dictionary of the Bible: An Illustrated Encyclopedia. New York: Abingdon, 1962 (4 vols.).

Peake's Commentary of the Bible. Revised edition edited by Matthew Black. London and New York: Thomas Nelson and Sons Ltd., 1962.

Index of Scriptures

229